I SEE WHAT YOU MEAN

Children at Work with Visual Information

STEVE MOLINE

Stenhouse Publishers
York, Maine

Stenhouse Publishers, 226 York Street, York, Maine 03909

Library of Congress Cataloging-in Publication-Data
Moline, Steve
    I see what you mean: children at work with visual information / Steve Moline.
    p.   cm.
    Includes bibliographical references and index.
    ISBN 1-57110-031-8 (alk. paper)
    1. Language arts—New South Wales. 2. Visual perception. 3. Visual education. I. Title.
LB1576.M58 1996
372.6'044—dc20   95-39708
                                                                                      CIP

Published simultaneously in Canada by   Designed by Norma van Rees
Pembroke Publishers Limited   Cover design by Cathy Hawkes
538 Hood Road   Manufactured in the United States of America on
Markham, Ontario L3R 3K9   acid-free paper
ISBN 1-55138-065-X   99 98 97 96 8 7 6 5 4 3 2 1

Acknowledgements

Australia
The author wishes to thank the students and staff of:
    Beechboro Primary School, WA
    Dobroyd Point Public School, Sydney, NSW
    Lethbridge Park Public School, Sydney, NSW
    Lithgow Public School, Lithgow, NSW
    Majura Primary School, Canberra, ACT
    Moulden Park School, Moulden, NT
    Orange East Public School, Orange, NSW
    Orange Public School, Orange, NSW
    Summer Hill Creek Public School, Orange, NSW.
Particular thanks to the following teachers whose students produced work that is included in this book and whose comments in some cases have been quoted in the text:
    Barbara Biddle, Marie Bloodworth, Ron Burton, Helen Campbell, Kerry Cambridge, Jim Canning, Christina Cannon, Michael Caraher, Dianne Constable, Chris Contos, Christine Curran, Peter Domazar, Mark Eyles, Ros Eyre, Francine Fogwell, Anne Kloczko, Franz Kunz, Kaye McFarnell, Anthea McLellan, Bronwyn Napper-Wilson, Jo Padgham, Clare Pritchard, Don Readett, Maree Robertson, Debbie Smith, Stella Smith, Debbie Steele, Kerry Stokes, Barbara Symons, Carolie Wilson, and Dorothy Woodside.
Thanks also to:
    Margaret Clyne, Tanya Dalgleish, Rachel Griffiths, Rhonda Jenkins, Julie McCowage, Viv Nicoll-Hatton, Dr. Brenda Parkes, Pamela Pearson, and Robyn Wild.

United States
The author wishes to thank the students and staff of:
    Harrison Avenue School, Harrison, NY; especially Claudette D'Arco, Billie Cohen, Dolores Genovese, Mary Nyland, and Chiara Michilli.
Thanks also to: Dr. Sandra Schwartz and Dr. John Jay Russell.

Publishers
The following publishers and copyright holders have granted permission to reproduce copyright material: Thomas Nelson Australia and Black Cockatoo Publishing for Chapter 3, Fig. 12B (anaconda diagram from *The Book of Animal Records* by David Drew) and Chapter 8, Fig. 2 (bird's eye view and map from *Somewhere in the Universe* by David Drew); Helicon Publishing for Chapter 4, Fig. 4 (Saturn V rocket from *Hutchinson Encyclopaedia*, 8th edition); Andromeda Oxford Limited for Chapter 8, Fig. 9 (weather map and key from *Concise Encyclopaedia of Science and Technology*, 1978); *The Times*, London and the Meteorological Office, London, for Chapter 8, Fig. 10 (weather maps, crown copyright, reproduced with the permission of Her Majesty's Stationery Office); the Weekly Review of Science and Technology, *New Scientist*, London, for Chapter 8, Fig. 11 (migration routes of wanderer butterfly); Taronga Zoo, Sydney and Coca-Cola Bottlers, Sydney, for Chapter 8, Fig. 12 (Zoo map); Grisewood and Dempsey Ltd. for Chapter 10, Fig. 9 (pages 52-53 from *The Story of Life on Earth / Tracing Its Origins and Development Through Time* by Michael Benton, published by Kingfisher Books, copyright © Grisewood and Dempsey Ltd. 1986 photographs copyright © Imitor, Biofotos).

Please note:
Macintosh is a registered trademark of Apple Computer, Inc.
ClarisWorks is a trademark of Claris Corporation.
PageMaker is a registered trademark of Aldus Corporation.
QuarkXPress is a registered trademark of Quark, Inc.

Contents

Chapter 1

Do I need this book?

This book is for the teacher who believes that literacy is more than reading stories; literacy also includes reading and writing information. Similarly, information literacy is more than communicating with words, because many information texts also include important visual elements, such as diagrams, graphs, maps and tables. To provide a complete literacy program, therefore, we need to include opportunities to draw information as well as to write it.

Many information texts use visual elements

Whether we are thinking of school textbooks, encyclopaedias, street maps, brochures, catalogues or environmental print such as road signs and shop fronts, we are surrounded by information texts which use pictures and symbols as well as words. We are reading these texts, both in books and beyond books, all the time. Students of all ages encounter these visual texts as frequently as adults do and are expected to understand them, both in school work and in everyday living. To reflect this range of literacies, a classroom program needs to include explicit instruction in how these texts work.

Many visual texts are accessible to all readers

One of the great advantages of visual texts, such as maps or diagrams, is that most of the information they provide is readily accessible to all readers, including very young children who are not yet fluent readers of words and older students whose first language is not English. Similarly, students who are judged to be "poor writers" (when asked to write exclusively in words) are sometimes discovered to be excellent communicators if they are allowed the option to write the same information in a visual form, for example, as a diagram, graph or map.

Many visual texts are complex, multilayered texts

However, visual texts are not simple texts. Reading and writing visual texts is not merely a transitional phase which is later discarded in favour of reading and writing words; visual text elements can be highly complex and are used extensively at all levels of learning through to university textbooks and postgraduate research papers. Visual texts are therefore not an academically "soft option" to verbal (words-only) texts, since they can be equally demanding to produce. Nor are they offered here as an alternative in place of verbal texts; rather the two are seen to be complementary, as is demonstrated by the combining of the two in many reference books and textbooks at all levels. Because a diagram can provide many layers of information and because a statistical graph can often be misinterpreted, it is necessary to provide explicit instruction in what these texts do and don't mean and how these texts make their meaning.

Visual texts communicate certain information more clearly than verbal texts

Consider a metropolitan street map, which provides the routes of thousands of possible journeys. We can use our visual literacy skills to calculate countless combinations of distances, directions, relative positions and even estimated journey times. If this visual information were converted to words alone, we would soon fill a book thousands of pages long. Such a book of directions would be vastly more difficult to access and the task of deciding between alternative routes would be made impossible by an apparent excess of detail. By providing the same information as a map, we can make the data more accessible, more memorable and more concise.

Which is the most appropriate text?

Students need opportunities to learn when one kind of text is more appropriate to their writing purpose than another. Choosing between making a map and writing a list of alternative routes or directions is one example. Similarly, students need practice in deciding whether a graph which summarises data will communicate the information more clearly than a list, a table or a string of sentences which provide the same content. Students will learn to choose the appropriate text for their purpose only if their literacy program provides both practice and explicit instruction in using a variety of kinds of text.

Visual texts are widely used in electronic media

In addition to the print media (books, newspapers, street maps, brochures etc.), visual texts are widely used in the growing array of electronic media with which students need to be familiar in order to be fully literate, both at school and elsewhere. These electronic information media include the Internet, CD-ROM and desktop publishing to name only a few. These media are encountered increasingly in the contexts of school, work and recreation and they rely heavily on a good understanding of how visual texts make meaning. While most of the student examples in this book are produced with pen and paper and relate especially to how printed media use visual texts, all of the forms discussed here are widely employed in the electronic information media as well.

Visual literacy is a life skill

We need visual literacy in order to get by in our everyday lives. The contexts in which visual texts are encountered include finding our way, following instructions, filling in government forms, applying for work, choosing consumer goods, planning a vacation and so on. The visual texts associated with these tasks include maps, street directories, street signs and shop fronts, video terminal displays, weather maps, printed forms, advertising, retailers' catalogues, product labels, travel brochures, airline schedules etc. All of these forms combine verbal and visual information to make meaning and all are organised along principles of graphic design that can be taught explicitly.

Positive outcomes

The intention of this book is not to provide busy work in writing diagrams, maps etc., for their own sake. But, by focusing students on questions such as how to match the form to the writer's purpose, we can show students that writing is above all communication with a reader who will expect our text to be accessible, memorable, concise and clear.

The strategies offered in the following pages are intended to:

- integrate literacy with other curriculum areas such as science and technology, human society, personal development and other key learning areas
- motivate students judged to be "non-writers" and "non-readers"
- develop initiative and independence in learning, especially in the areas of research and writing
- give support and confidence to those students whose strengths lie in visual perception (including visualising research data and their own solutions) or who communicate well by drawing objects, mapping concepts and organising content using graphic design

- develop thinking skills such as selecting and combining strategies to solve problems and to initiate new solutions to writing tasks
- combine verbal and visual literacies to make an integrated text.

Chapter 2

Reading and writing information

When we are teaching students to read we are not only showing them how to read, we are also telling them what reading is like and what reading is for.

If we spend most of our day reading stories with students and asking them to read or write stories, we are telling our students that most of what they will read in everyday life will be stories. But most of what we read and write in everyday life are not stories or poems or rhymes; most of what adults read and write each day are information texts.

What do we read and write in a day?

Consider what you read (and wrote) yesterday. Make a list, trying to recall everything — not just in the classroom, where you read and wrote as a professional teacher of literacy, but everything you read and wrote at home and in between.

Your list might begin like this (Fig. 1):

Fig. 1 ♦ "What did I read and write yesterday?"

Read/ Write	Item	Purpose	Text
R	newspaper	check headlines	news report
R	newspaper	check weather	map, summary
W	message	ask neighbour to walk dog	letter, request
etc.			

Compare your list with what Alice read and wrote (Fig. 2). Although everybody's list will be different, there are likely to be some points in common: most of the reading and writing we do is information and in all the lists there is a wide range of items, purposes and texts. Much of what we read are visual texts (such as advertising) as well as verbal texts (such as a newspaper article).

Fig. 2 ♦ What Alice read and wrote in a day
(Alice is a primary school teacher with one child, Nick.)

Read/Write	Item	Purpose	Text
R/W	diary	check day's schedule, add "phone Jo"	journal entries
R	phone list	arrange Sue B. to drive Nick to soccer	alphabetical list
W	message	remind Nick to feed Sugar, I'll be late	instruction, request (letter)
W	shopping list	for Nick to do after school	list arranged in groups
R/W	field trip form	allow Nick's school to take Nick to Mudgee	official form, Q&A
R/W	notice board (staff room)	check news, notices etc., and add name to roster	table, letter, bulletin, advertising
R	aspirin pack	check dosage — headache	instructions
R	crossword	relax	cloze exercise?
R/W	phone book	check Jo's number: come to inservice?	alphabetical list, note
R	street map	check location of inservice	map, index
R	autobank	withdraw cash	questions, instructions
R	catalogue	catch up on new picture books	captions, photos, lists
R/W	handout	to follow workshop activity	interview, graph, table
W	notes	to remember points in workshop	summary, diagrams
R	pizza pack	decide: do I want to eat this stuff? how long in the microwave?	list (ingredients) instructions
R	N's homework	Nick needs reassurance	report, labelled diagram
R	TV guide	what's on?	chronological list, table
R	novel	relax	fiction

In Alice's list there are more than twenty different styles of information or information print, but only one example of fiction. She read information for different purposes:

- for enjoyment (the crossword)
- for short-term use (the autobank, the aspirin pack)
- for long-term learning (the workshop handout).

Often these purposes are combined. A magazine article may offer both enjoyment and long-term knowledge. It is easy to say that fiction is for pleasure, while nonfiction is for learning; that is, for "work". But our information reading, both in the classroom and out of it, often combines enjoyment with learning.

Reading information

How we read depends on our purpose for reading

There is more than one way to read a book. We can read it from front to back, intently, leaving nothing out. We can browse through the pictures. We can search for one or two facts only, picking out only the straws we need from the haystack of information. We can scan, sample, skip and skim. How we read depends on our purpose for reading.

Consider, for example, the differences between how we read a biography; that is, when we read it "for the story" and how we read the same book when we wish to locate specific information:

When we read "for the story":
- we want to read the whole text
- we start at the front and end at the back
- we read from top to bottom and from left to right
- if we put the book down, we pick it up later at the point in the narrative where we left off
- the verbal narrative of a biography does not need the pictures to make its meaning
- the first line is the gateway through which we enter the text
- completion of the narrative is part of the satisfaction of reading it.

But when we read selectively to locate specific information:
- we can choose to read only part of the text
- we may start at the front, the back or somewhere in between; that is, we can choose the gateway through which we enter the text, for example:
  — the contents page
  — the index
  — the headings
  — the pictures and captions
- the visual elements (photographs, diagrams, maps etc.) can be read for meaning, even when they contain few words or no words
- the diagrams, maps, graphs etc., sometimes need to be read:
  — bottom to top
  — right to left
  — in a circular, apparently random or zigzag way, depending on its design and our own purpose in reading it
- if we pick up the book later, it may be for an entirely different purpose, so we don't need to find the place where we left off

- we sometimes stroll through an information text backwards and we still make sense of the parts we read
- sometimes the words make incomplete sense without the visual elements that accompany them; words and image together make the meaning
- we read what we need and often we write (we make notes) while we read.

As readers we are free to choose how we read an information text, such as a biography. We can choose to follow the author's pathway, that is, to read "the whole story"; or we can choose to read the same text selectively, choosing our own pathways.

What is special about selective reading?

If we teach children that *all* reading is "reading for the story", we overlook many key strategies that we employ when reading selectively. Some of these strategies include scanning, skimming, accessing the text through the index, using headings as signposts to the information we want or just strolling through the pictures in order to orientate ourselves in the text.

These selective reading strategies depend on the purposes we bring as readers to the text and the special kind of interactive relationship the reader has with an information text.

We can choose to read only part of the text.

If we are looking for a single fact in an indexed street directory, we scan for one line in the alphabetical list of streets and we look for one set of coordinates on one map on one page of the book. The procedure has more in common with selecting alternatives from a computer menu than with reading narrative. The reader is using the book instrumentally.

We may start at the front, the back or somewhere in between.

In order to access information from a reference book, we may choose to enter through the contents page at the front, the index at the back or we may wish to browse through the pictures, captions or headings. There is no obligation to read all the pages or to read them in the sequence in which they are arranged.

The visual elements (photographs, diagrams, maps etc.) can be read for meaning, even when they contain no (or few) words.

A sequence of photographs showing the life cycle of a caterpillar, for example, can be interpreted as meaningful text even by very young readers. A builder's plan of a house, even if it contains no words, can be read for information about relative sizes, distances, positions, elevations etc., of the rooms, fittings and furnishings. An example of such a "wordless text" is Fig. 3, which is an account of how to obtain, plant and grow seeds.

Fig. 3 ◆ A "wordless text" by John (grade 1/2)
John has made this account of how to obtain, plant and grow seeds, without using words to explain this process.

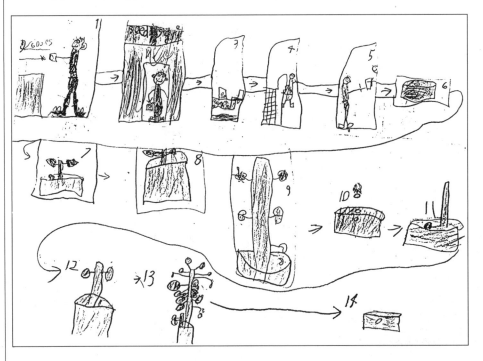

This process is explained by John (grade 1/2) without words. When asked to write a caption, John provided a verbal text which supported and added to the diagram (Fig. 4).

Fig. 4 ◆ John's caption for Fig. 3
John did not complete the captions for steps 11-14. However, the wordless graphic in Fig. 3 makes sense without words.

1 a seed was bought at a store
2 the person who bought the seed went out of the store
3 then drove the son to school
4 and when the mum gave the son the seeds the mum drove off
5 the son gave the seeds to the teacher
6 the seed was planted, it grew
7 in 2 months it will sprout
8 it will grow bigger
9 then it will drop beans and seeds
10 the stem will grow

However, some information appears only in the drawings and not in the words. For example, the growing pattern and the structure of the bean plant is shown in pictures *11–13* and the cyclical nature of the process is indicated when the plant produces seed again in picture *14*. Yet these steps *11–14* are not accompanied by captions.

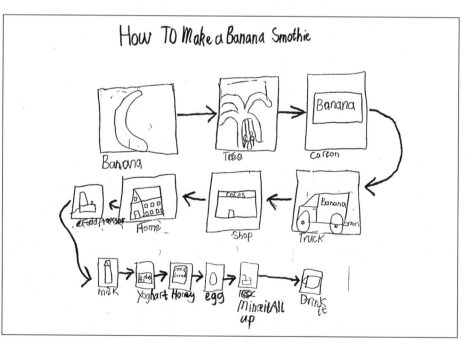

TIMELINE FOR KATIE

Visual texts may be read from bottom to top or from right to left.

This is more commonplace than you may think. In Katie's time line (Fig. 5) we have a choice of starting at birth and reading Katie's life as a narrative (from left to right). However, if our purpose is to find out what happened to Katie last year, we would choose to start at the right and read the text "backwards". The labels on this time line are written sideways and to read them more comfortably the reader needs to turn the page 90° so that 1992 is at the top and 1984 is at the bottom. Therefore, if we wish to follow the time line in chronological order, we must read the text from bottom to top. In each case, our purpose dictates the direction we take through the text.

Diagrams may also be read in a zigzag way.

Dino's diagram "How To Make a Banana Smoothie" (Fig. 6) is such an example. In this case, we follow a process through a "meandering river" structure which zigzags down the page.

Fig. 6 ♦ A zigzag pathway
Many flow diagrams, time lines, "story maps" and other texts invite the reader to take a pathway through the text, using arrows as signposts. In the case of "How To Make a Banana Smoothie", Dino (grade 3) directs the reader through a sequence of stages which explain where the ingredients come from (in the top two rows) and then instructs us (in the last row) how to make the smoothie.

How To Make a Banana Smothie

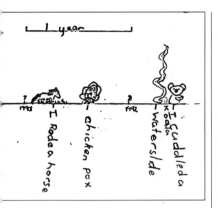

Another zigzag pathway is "hidden" in the text "Today's Weather" by Jordie (Fig. 7). Although there are no arrows to make the pathways explicit, we are required to move back and forth between the key (or "code") and the map in order to make sense of the symbols in the map. A similar zigzag reading pattern typically links a visual text with its supporting caption, particularly where a caption defines terms used in the text it accompanies. In the case of Fig. 7, the map helps to explain the caption: Jordie's weather statements on the left use abbreviations (such as "NT 32 Fine") which are defined by the map.

Fig. 7 ♦ "Today's Weather" by Jordie (grade 5/6)
In order to make meaning from this text, the reader traces a pathway back and forth between the key (or "code") and the map.

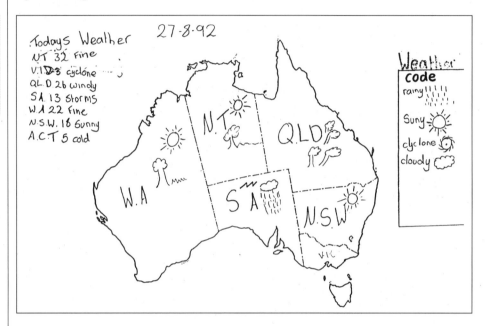

Other diagrams can be read in a circular or apparently random way.

On a map, for example, all the words seem to be of equal importance and can be read in any order. Each connection between a part of the drawing and its label is a self-contained text element; so the text makes equally good sense, regardless of the order in which we read the labels. The reading sequence is dictated by the reader's purpose. Many visual texts work like this; they make sense and are often rich in meaning, yet they do not provide us with explicit directions concerning what to read next. Many visual texts (not just maps) can also be read in this apparently random way.

If we pick up the book later, it may be for an entirely different purpose, so we don't need to find the place where we left off.

Consider how different our reading strategies will be in response to the following questions, "Do I understand the writer's argument?" and "Is the writer aware of the most recent statistics?". In the first case, we need to read the whole argument in the sequence the writer sets it out, to fulfil our purpose; in the second case we need only look at one column in one table on one page.

We sometimes stroll through an information text backwards and we still make sense of the parts we read.
This strategy applies, for example, to recreational reading, such as browsing in a magazine. It also applies to the way we read a book we have just picked up for the first time. In this situation, we often scan the pictures, if it is an illustrated reference book, in order to orientate ourselves in the book. This orientation is partly recreational and partly a data-gathering activity, in which we are assessing the text's scope and usefulness to our purpose.

Sometimes the words make incomplete sense without the visual elements that accompany them; words and image together make the meaning.
This applies, for example, to a map, where the visual elements (such as the colours, the symbols, the roads and coastlines) and the words or numerals (such as the place names or the grid numbers) are fully understood only when they are interpreted together. If we move the names on the map we change the map's meaning; in fact we can falsify information on a map simply by repositioning the words. Position is therefore a part of a word's meaning in some visual texts. Likewise we can make nonsense of a map by transposing the symbols for shipwrecks and mountains.

Finally, we read what we need and often we write (we make notes) while we read.
When we read for a specific short-term purpose (such as finding a number in the phone book) or for a long-term learning goal (such as research), we are extracting the one piece of data we need out of a large organised source of data most of which we may never read. And in order to remember this one fact (whether it is the height of a mountain or the address of your dentist) we need to record it. Often we read information with pen in hand. In Alice's list (Fig. 2) about one-third of her reading activities also involved writing.

Writing information

There is an important message for how we teach writing in this discussion about selective reading. When students write an information text, they need to keep in mind that their readers will often want to read their text selectively; they therefore need to consider:

- How can I help my readers to find the information they need?
- What is the clearest, most memorable way in which to present my information?
- How can the design of my text support the reader?

Questions such as these invite the student to consider:

- How can I organise and signpost my information to help my readers find their way through my text?
- Is the information I wish to write best expressed as a map, diagram, graph or verbal text; or a combination of all four?
- Do I need to explain my diagram with labels or with a caption?
- Can I highlight, separate or connect parts of my text using colour coding, columns, box outlines etc.?

Graphic design

In order to organise the information and support the reader of our information text, we need to consider some of the elements of graphic design. Graphic design is part of communication and is relevant to writing of all information texts whether they are newspapers, advertising, encyclopaedias, cookbooks or textbooks; that is, whether their function is to instruct, report, explain or persuade.

Good design contributes to a text's meaning and helps the reader to access the text. Some of the features of graphic design and the purposes to which these features are put are listed below.

We can:	By using:
highlight	colour
connect	arrows or numbers
group into hierarchies	headings and subheadings
organise	columns
separate	white space
cross reference	asterisks(*) and footnotes

By using graphic design features such as these we can organise the information we write into integrated texts.

Integrated texts

A text which combines paragraphs, headings, visual elements and design features can be seen as an integrated text. A text will be integrated only if its parts support, explain or give context to one another.

Given some explicit guidance concerning possible visual texts to use and how to design them, Helen (grade 3/4) produced an integrated text on rabbits (Fig. 8) which combines some of the elements of a published information book. Helen has employed a heading and several subheadings. Each subheading has its paragraphed text and some of these are extended by visual texts, labels and captions. The "Description" works like an introduction and the piece ends with a "Bibliography".

Fig. 8 ♦ Helen's text about rabbits

Helen (grade 3/4) has constructed an integrated text which combines a heading and several subheadings, paragraphed texts, a caption, a photograph, a picture glossary ("carrot, lettuce, celery") and a cross section (the burrow). The design elements which integrate these text elements include the box around the whole page, the box which links the main heading to the texts below it and the white space separating the two columns of verbal text.

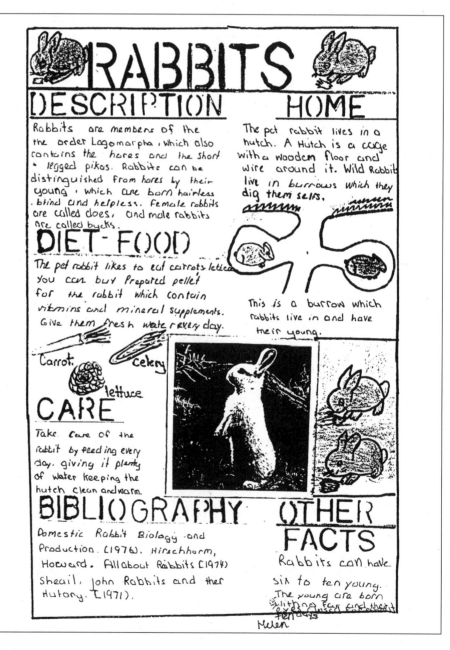

Helen's verbal texts include:
- the main heading "Rabbits"
- the subheadings "Description", "Home" etc.
- the paragraphed texts which follow each subheading
- the caption "This is a burrow ... ".

Helen's visual texts include:
- a picture glossary (with labels)
- a cross section (with a caption).

Helen's page design includes:
- the boxes, rules and white space which link or separate the text elements.

Helen's text is an integrated text because the visual texts support (or explain) the paragraphed texts, which in turn offer generalisations that give the visual texts their context. For example:
- The cross section of the burrow shows how the burrow is structured into rooms joined by tunnels. This is additional information which supports the paragraphed text about the rabbit's "home".
- The caption links this cross section to the paragraphed text above it, while extending the information with the additional generalisation that rabbits give birth inside the burrow.
- The picture glossary ("carrot, celery, lettuce") itemises the rabbit's diet, supporting the list of items in the paragraph above it.
- The box around the heading and the rabbit symbols inside the box work together to establish the main heading (the name of the theme) of this page. The whole page is boxed to isolate it as a thematically self-contained text.

Writing and drawing

Helen's text about rabbits combines verbal elements (the paragraphs and headings) with visual elements (the diagrams), to form an integrated text. Since a significant part of an integrated text lies in its visual elements, Helen's ability to draw is as important as her ability to write. Drawing can sometimes be neglected or treated as an add-on reward or afterthought in the classroom. Even in classrooms where there are many opportunities to draw there is sometimes the assumption that in the end drawing is not really as important (as useful, as serious) as writing.

This attitude sometimes takes the form of an instruction to provide a written report, "and if you have time left over, do a drawing". There are a number of messages implied in this remark:
- drawing is not as necessary as writing, because it is optional

- writing is real work and is valued for that reason; whereas drawing is fun but is of little value
- drawing can at best illustrate (or at worst decorate) writing.

But we have just seen that drawing is integral to the meaning of information texts and in this context it is not the same as "doing art". When we look at Helen's text about rabbits, the diagrams are functioning as text elements that communicate meaning; they refine, clarify, itemise and extend the meanings of the words.

Matching text and purpose

If we expect students to produce visual texts, then we need to help them to decide which is the most appropriate (the most useful, clear, concise or memorable) form to choose. Students need practice in asking, for example:

- Is this information best presented as a list or as a diagram?
- Is this best explained in a paragraph or as a table?
- Can I say this better as a set of instructions or as a sequence of numbered diagrams?

When selecting which text is most useful (to the writer and to the reader), it can be helpful to discuss a range of possible text forms with the students before they embark on a final draft. To enable them to match text to purpose, provide the students with some examples of different kinds of text; these could be selected from a checklist such as Fig. 9.

Fig. 9 ◆ Which text? Matching purpose, topic and text

Purpose	Topic	Visual text
to explain	how glass is recycled	• flow diagram (steps in recycling process) • pie graph (how many bottles are recycled?) • table (items that can be recycled)
to instruct	how to make a kite	• picture glossary (materials needed) • flow diagram (method/procedure)
to report	Tyrannosaurus rex	• scale diagram (size of animal) • cutaway (to show skeleton inside) • tree (evolution of carnivorous dinosaurs) • bird's eye view (of habitat) • context map (location of fossils) • flow maps (continental drift)
to recount	field trip to the zoo	• time line (our day at the zoo) • map (of zoo) • column graph (how much the animals eat) • web (zoo jobs)
to persuade	"smoking: quit for life"	• photograph (overflowing ashtray) • line graph (cancer deaths since 1960) • cross section (smoker's lungs) • bar graph (men and women smokers)

When using a checklist such as this, remind the students that:
- the best format is often the simplest and clearest
- visual texts tend to summarise and highlight, whereas verbal texts tend to be more comprehensive and detailed
- visual texts can be used to support with explanations or examples the generalisations in paragraphed text
- paragraphed texts often provide a context for the visual texts
- the purpose is to make meaning, not to "do a graph" or "have a lesson in writing diagrams".

In planning a unit of study which requires the students to write information, it is helpful to make an outline such as Fig. 9, to ensure that the students are given the opportunity to consider what options are available to them and to select the best text for their purpose. Choosing the best text requires us to consider both our own needs as writers (does it help me organise the data?) and also our reader's needs (is it accessible, clear, memorable, supportive?).

Students also need to have ready access to examples of these kinds of text, which can be displayed as wall charts in the room. You may be displaying some of these visual texts in your classroom already. For example:

Time lines	—	prehistory, local history
Graphs	—	local weather (temperature, rainfall)
Tables	—	calendar, classroom roster
Diagrams	—	human body, parts of a plant
Maps	—	world, city, neighbourhood

Graphic design is discussed in more detail in Chapter 10.

Recomposing

Recomposing often happens when students attempt to match text to purpose. It is both an effective research strategy and a powerful aid to comprehension.

1 Ask students to read the information in one format (such as an encyclopaedia entry), but to write their own account using a different format (such as a diagram, table, graph or map).

2 Say to the students, "You have to find a different way to express the same information".

3 Allow students to compare how other groups solved this problem.

This strategy prevents students from copying out "slabs from the encyclopaedia", since they cannot write down the information in the same form in which they have read it. Because they cannot copy the form of the text, they are obliged to internalise the key facts that have now to be presented in a new format.

You will be already familiar with recomposing if you have ever asked students to make a story map of a narrative they have just read, or a sociogram of its main characters. It is equally effective with information research. Whenever we ask students to read information in one format and then write it in another format, we are asking them to "recompose" the information. We will meet this term often in the following chapters.

Teaching practices: reading and writing information

- Offer a variety of reading purposes, including reading of whole books and selective reading for specific information.
- Consider the most appropriate verbal or visual text for each task.
- Set meaningful purposes for reading information texts; avoid "doing visual texts" for their own sake.
- Demonstrate for students how to "read what you need": scan, sample, skip and skim.
- Provide real situations in which students need to make notes while reading.
- Use information big books to show children how we interpret graphs, tables, indexes etc., and how we make notes while using information texts.
- Give students practice in asking themselves, "What is the best text for what I have to say?"; that is, what is the clearest, most concise, most memorable and most supportive form in which to say it?
- Display examples of visual texts in your classroom.

Chapter

Simple diagrams

Diagrams can be thought of simply as labelled pictures, but they are usually more than this. A better explanation of a diagram might be that it is a graphic text in which:

- the illustration and the words work together to make the meaning
- the illustration simplifies, generalises or symbolises the subject, rather than shows us its surface appearance (such as its colour or texture).

Perhaps the simplest diagrams are:

- pictures with labels (picture glossaries)
- pictures with a scale (scale diagrams).

A *picture glossary* (Fig. 1A) helps the reader to identify, differentiate or define items within a group or parts of a whole.

A *scale diagram* (Fig. 1B) is a picture of a subject with a scale beside it which indicates its size, mass or distance etc.

Figs. 1A and 1B ♦ Simple diagrams
Fig. 1A is a picture glossary which defines parts of a whole. Fig. 1B is a scale diagram which shows the size of a whale shark using a scale (1 cm = 1 m).

Fig. 1A ♦ A picture glossary
Parts of a honey bee by Jodi (grade 2)

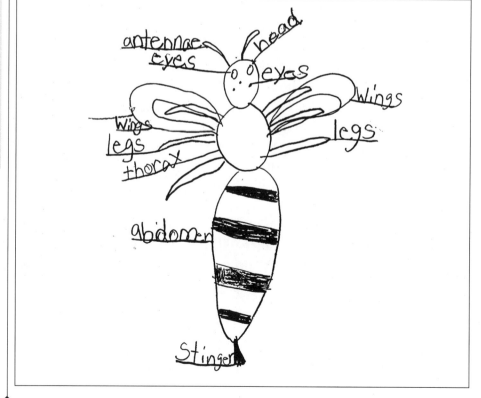

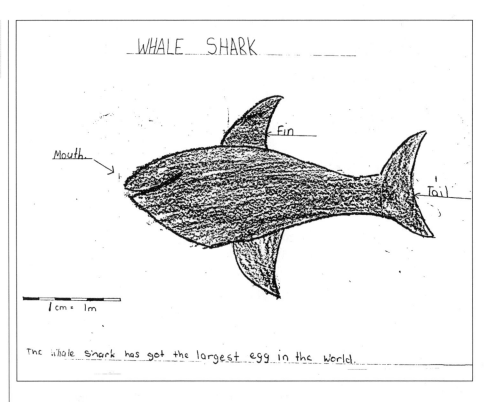

WHALE SHARK

Fin

Mouth

Tail

1 cm = 1m

The whale shark has got the largest egg in the world.

Jodi's picture glossary of a honeybee (Fig. 1A) provides more information than a list of the same words used in the labels. Her diagram shows us the relative size and position of each item and the symmetrical structure of the insect. Students can be encouraged to notice how much graphic information is in a diagram like this by asking them:

- How many legs are on each side?
- Has Jodi drawn the right number of wings and antennae?
- Which is bigger, the head or the thorax?
- Match up the items on the left with the items on the right of its body.

Sarah's scale diagram of a whale shark (Fig. 1B) includes only three labels, but the scale allows us to ask the students questions such as:

- How long is its fin? How big is its tail?
- Would a whale shark fit inside our classroom?

By asking these questions we draw the students' attention to the fact that much of the information is in the visual elements of the diagram. Students can also be asked to write down "all the things the picture tells us". The visual information, when written out as verbal (words-only) text, would quickly fill several pages.

Picture glossaries

In a picture glossary the labels name parts of the picture, while the picture helps to define the labels.

Using picture glossaries

Purposes:
- to define subjects or concepts visually
- to show relationships between parts of a subject
- to define differences, varieties and categories; to classify subgroups
- to organise vocabulary lists into meaningful groups and sequences.

Contexts:
- any subject about which it is useful to name its parts and understand their relative positions
- science: animal groups, body parts, parts of a plant etc.
- technology: naming of working parts (machines, systems etc.)
- society: naming of varieties (kinds of housing, food, transport etc.)
- health: human body, food groups.

Outcomes:
- uses drawing skills to communicate information
- can define terms by placing them correctly on a diagram
- can name the key parts of a subject using labels
- summarises information pictorially.

Examples in big books:
Hidden Animals, pp. 5–17 (small animals and insects).
Small Worlds, pp. 2–3 (solar system).
Caterpillar Diary, p. 8 (parts of a caterpillar).
What Should I Use?, pp. 4–16 (simple machines).
Misbuildings, pp. 2–16 (built environment, transport)
Rainforests of Australia, p. 15 (insects).
Caterpillars, pp. 4–9 (emperor moth and catepillar).

Introducing picture glossaries

Here are three ways to introduce students to using picture glossaries successfully:

Using big books

Use big books that include picture glossaries to show students how these diagrams work and what they tell us. A list of suitable examples is in the table above.

Sorting and naming

1 Collect a number of small, miscellaneous objects (or ask the students to do this). They can be "anything smaller than your hand", for example, match box, paper clip, bus ticket, pencil, pebble, feather, shell, wishbone etc.
2 Working in groups of three or four, the students discuss what each item is called. They then arrange each item with its name, which they can either write as a label, a list or a table.

3 Ask the students to find things in common among the items. The students group the items, draw them and label them, as in Amy's picture glossary of deciduous leaves in Fig. 2.

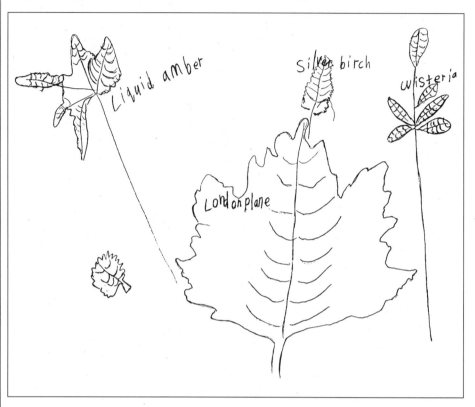

Amy's class was working on a season theme which led to a discussion of which trees lose their leaves. Her teacher collected a number of deciduous leaves and displayed them (with their names) under clear contact film as a wall chart. Amy's teacher comments:

> The children collected a leaf from each deciduous tree or creeper in the playground. They attempted to draw and label the leaves they had found (using the examples on the wall). There was some discussion after their first attempts, drawing attention to the need for more detail.
>
> — Grade 1/2 teacher (BS)

Amy's text is one of the first attempts. She has shown just enough detail to indicate differences in the venation of these leaves, which are largely defined by their outline. In these two respects, Amy has produced a diagram (not simply a picture) in which details have been selected (highlighted or omitted) for their information content. Amy has had to decide what is essentially "wisteria-like" in order to draw the wisteria leaf. What she has produced is a diagram (rather than a "drawing") because the subject is simplified and generalised.

Drawing details

You can also introduce picture glossaries as a game:

1 Bring a familiar object into the classroom, such as a bicycle.

2 The students take turns to draw on a large sheet of paper (which everyone can see) a magnified picture of any small detail on the bicycle; it might be a row of cogs, two links in the chain or a valve.

3 The rest of the class have to guess what the detail is and the first person to guess the item (and to write its correct name) takes over and draws another detail. In a short time the students have produced a picture glossary (Fig. 3).

This game develops the students' powers of observation and challenges them to use accurate and appropriate technical language. The game of drawing, guessing and naming parts could be played with a vacuum cleaner, a caterpillar, a radio/cassette player, a sunflower etc. On a field trip to a fire station, a building site or an animal sanctuary, you could play this game to help students observe details. In each case the students are producing a picture glossary.

Working with picture glossaries

Diagrams as glossaries

Labelled diagrams work like glossaries and they can be a more powerful tool than vocabulary lists. In Fig. 3 the words are supported by the pictures which help to define or explain the meanings of the words especially for very young students or those students who are learning English as a second language. Help students to see the full meaning of a text like this by asking them to explain what a valve or a sprocket is. Their definitions will be derived from close observation of the picture: "Sprockets are the small triangular-shaped cogs on the wheel you turn with the pedals" (Alison, grade 4).

Fig. 3 ◆ Drawing and naming details
A bicycle was brought into the classroom and the students were asked to draw and name parts of it.

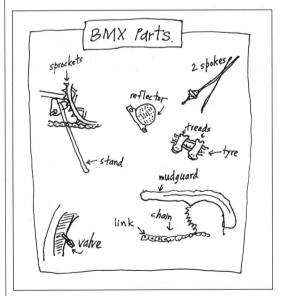

Diagrams as summaries

After reading a book about large machines, Elizabeth (grade 1) was asked to summarise what she had discovered about one of the machines in the book using a picture glossary. Her diagram of a compactor (Fig. 4) labels some of the features of this road-making vehicle, giving prominence to the "roller that flattens the dirt".

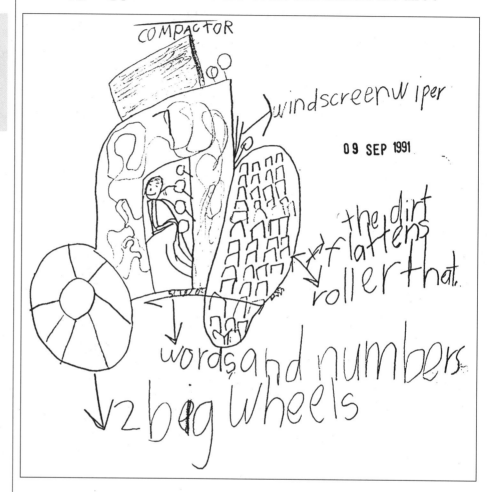

Drawing a diagram in such a context is rather like making notes during or after reading a text. This diagram is a way of making notes which has certain advantages over simply making a list of words. For example, as well as itemising the parts of the vehicle, Elizabeth can show where they are in relation to each other and can (without words) emphasise the central role played by the driver who operates a set of levers. In both these cases, the pictorial part of the diagram is providing information that is not provided by the words.

In order to produce this text, Elizabeth needed to reread the original text, study the picture (a photograph) and recompose the information as a diagram. The activity is at the same time a comprehension task and a preparation for further writing, since the next step might be to recompose the diagram as a paragraph about compactors.

Diagrams that show structure

A picture glossary has another main advantage over a simple list of words (such as a word bank or theme list), in that a diagram can show the relationships between the parts and the structure of the whole. This is useful, for example, when working on topics such as how machines or systems work or animal and plant parts.

Christy's diagram of a bean plant (Fig. 5) does more than list the parts of a plant. Since the names are presented as labels for a diagram which is drawn to scale (the stem is "about 23 cm long"), her diagram also tells us:

• the relative and actual sizes of all the parts of the plant
• the relative positions of the key parts of the plant
• the structure of the roots, leaf venation and bud inflorescence.

The diagram even tells us in what order the soil and gravel should be placed in the pot.

Fig. 5 ♦ "A Bean Plant"
Christy (grade 5) has produced an integrated text which includes heading, paragraphed text and graphics (combining a picture glossary with a cross section) that recounts a classroom activity growing a plant.

There is a difference between asking students to label a pre-existing diagram (in a worksheet, for example) and asking them to draw as well as label the diagram. This is because a large part of the understanding that students gain from these texts lies in reconstructing the pictorial elements of the diagram. In the picture glossary "Bones of the hand" (Fig. 6) for example, Stephen and Jim were required to draw accurately the shapes, sizes and positions of the bones, not simply to name them.

Fig. 6 ♦ "Bones of the hand"
Stephen (grade 6) and Jim (grade 5) worked together to produce this picture glossary of the bones of the right hand. Drawing the bones' shapes and positions is as important as naming the parts.

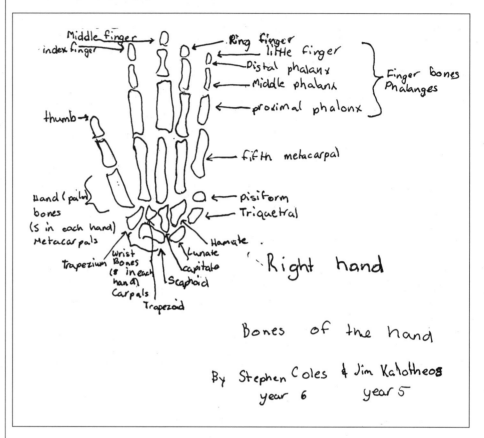

In a kindergarten classroom the same theme of the human skeleton was approached in this sequence:
- handling a life-sized (plastic) human skeleton
- drawing a skeleton diagram and labelling it
- labelling a pre-existing diagram.

After handling and studying the life-sized skeleton, Helen (kindergarten) produced Fig. 7 and after discussion her teacher asked Helen to label the parts of a diagram of a skeleton (Fig. 8). Her teacher comments:

We had looked at a life-sized skeleton and talked about different bones before the children went to various free activities. Helen sat down and drew a skeleton and (on my suggestion) labelled it (Fig. 7). The next day she brought to class a book on the body and again produced her own version. I then gave the children a stencil with instructions to label as many parts as possible (Fig. 8).

— Kindergarten teacher (KC)

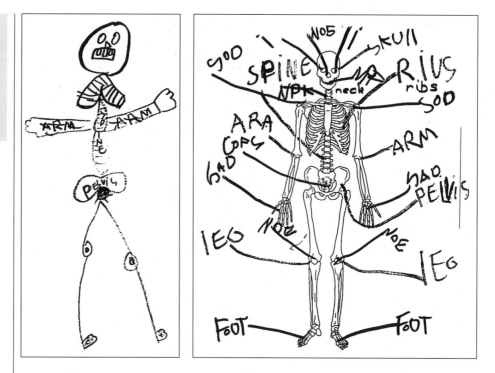

There is clearly more verbal information (that is, more labels) in
the second diagram. By ensuring that all parts appear in the picture,
the students are more likely to label all of its parts. However, the
first diagram, which has less words and which is less accurate, is
nevertheless the more challenging task as a learning activity, since
Helen has had to reconstruct the subject pictorially herself, by
showing the relationships between the head, ribs, spine, arms,
pelvis and legs.

In another kindergarten classroom, the students were asked to
make a picture glossary of an ant (Fig. 9) after studying large colour
photographs and using a word bank arranged as a wall chart.

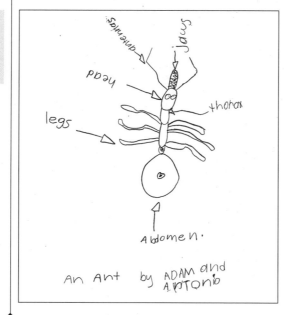

The teacher comments:

In a unit on living things the children and I had been sharing books about ants and attempting to establish an ant colony. While discussing types of ants suitable for our colony we began to identify parts they had in common. We studied some ants we had collected, as well as some pictures and some enlarged photographs and photocopies.

The children then made the diagrams of "an ant" and labelled them from a word bank prepared during discussion. It was working in pairs which made this writing activity so interesting, whether it was describing what they were doing, deciding what needed changing (for example, size, shape etc.) or helping each other with words needed on the word chart. Most children did this by recognition of initial and final consonants and other phonic-based strategies.

— Kindergarten/grade 1 teacher (CP)

Diagrams with keys

In order to make the meaning clear most of these diagrams use arrows or lines to connect labels with pictures. However, lines and arrows can interfere with the picture at times and an alternative is to identify the parts, for example by symbols or colours, and to provide a key explaining them. In the case of Jennifer's picture glossary of a honey bee (Fig. 10), both connecting lines and colours have been used. The key has been arranged as a table in which the colours have been named rather than simply employed as patches. The structure of the key was devised by the child. Her teacher gave students the opportunity to study how this kind of text worked before asking them to attempt their own:

The children had been working on a unit on honeybees ...

Together we labelled an enlarged poster of a honeybee and displayed this in the room several days before the children attempted their own diagrams.

When we were ready to begin using this strategy, I removed the labelled honeybee poster and replaced it with just a plain honeybee poster. On chart paper we listed all of the parts of a honeybee. The children were given plain paper and asked to make their own diagram.

During the next session they decided on adding a colour key to their diagrams. Each child devised a different kind of key.

— Grade 2 teacher (MN)

antenna
compound eyes
small eyes
Legs
wings
stinger

head
thorax
abdomen

_Bee.

color key

head	orngen
thorax	pink
abdomen	blue
antenna	yellow
compound er	brown
small eyes	brown
Legs	black
wing	gray
stinger	green

Fig. 10 ♦ A colour key
Jennifer (grade 2) has indicated
the parts of her diagram using a
colour key as well as connecting
lines.

Scale diagrams

A scale diagram is a picture of a subject with a scale beside it which indicates its size, mass, temperature, distance etc. Scale diagrams help students to imagine very large quantities or microscopic details, either by putting remote subjects in a familiar context (such as comparing a dinosaur's size with a cat's, as in Fig. 11A) or drawing the subject to scale with a standard unit of measurement (such as showing the size of the planet Neptune using a kilometre scale, as in Fig. 11B).

Figs. 11A and 11B ♦ Scale diagrams: conventional units and picture units
Using a picture unit (Fig. 11A) helps put unfamiliar subjects in a familiar context. Using conventional units of measurement (Fig. 11B) allows for a more exact measurement of the subject.

Fig. 11A ♦ Using a picture unit
The approximate size of a Saltopus dinosaur is indicated by drawing it to the same scale as a house cat.

Fig. 11B ♦ Using a conventional unit (km)
The exact size of the planet Neptune is indicated by using a scale in standard units of measurement.

Picture units and conventional units

In some of these scale diagrams there are two units of measurement:
- a picture unit, such as the cat in Fig. 11A
- a conventional unit, such as the km scale in Fig. 11B.

Picture units, though less accurate than conventional units, provide a more familiar context and are often more effective in helping students to imagine the size of the subject.

Conventional units of measurement are more accurate but sometimes rather abstract and when dealing in large numbers the subject can still be difficult to imagine.

Which measuring unit you choose depends on your purpose. Both kinds of measuring units should be used when students are asked to design and make scale diagrams.

Introducing scale diagrams

When young children discuss photographs of insects, dinosaurs, giant snakes or planets they often want to ask about the size of what they are looking at. This is because many photographs do not give us any clues to their scale and in order to interpret the text children often need to know about its size. Scale diagrams provide this important information, which is often missing from other kinds of diagrams or from photographs.

Estimation

Ask the students to estimate the length (or area, mass or volume) of the subject in the photograph. You could put this question in many ways:

- Is it bigger than a cat?
- Could it fit through the door?
- How many could you fit on top of a pin head?
- If the Earth was the size of this golf ball, how big do you think Jupiter would be?
- If it was standing on a giant seesaw, how many people would need to stand on the other end to balance it?
  — and so on.

It will help the students if they draw a sketch of some of these answers, which may be estimates of the subject's length, height or mass.

Measurement

In order to produce scale diagrams the students need to find ways to express the subject's length, height, area, mass, temperature, volume etc. They should be encouraged to adapt or invent suitable ways of indicating scale.

In the case of the small dinosaur (Fig. 11A) the students can measure the length of their cat with a tape measure (or agree on a typical length of a cat) and calculate the height and length of the Saltopus dinosaur in standard units (centimetres). In estimating the size of the large dinosaur (Fig. 12A) a grid was marked in square metres, so that both height and length could be calculated from the diagram. In the case of the snake (Fig. 12B) the students can use a set of bathroom scales to measure the mass of an adult; they can then calculate the mass of the anaconda. Speed or temperature can be indicated using specially designed scales (Figs. 12C and 12D).

There are many different kinds of
scales that are suitable for
indicating size, area,
temperature, speed etc. Allow
students to experiment with these
scales and to invent or adapt
others.

**Fig. 12A ♦ Using a grid to
indicate height and length**

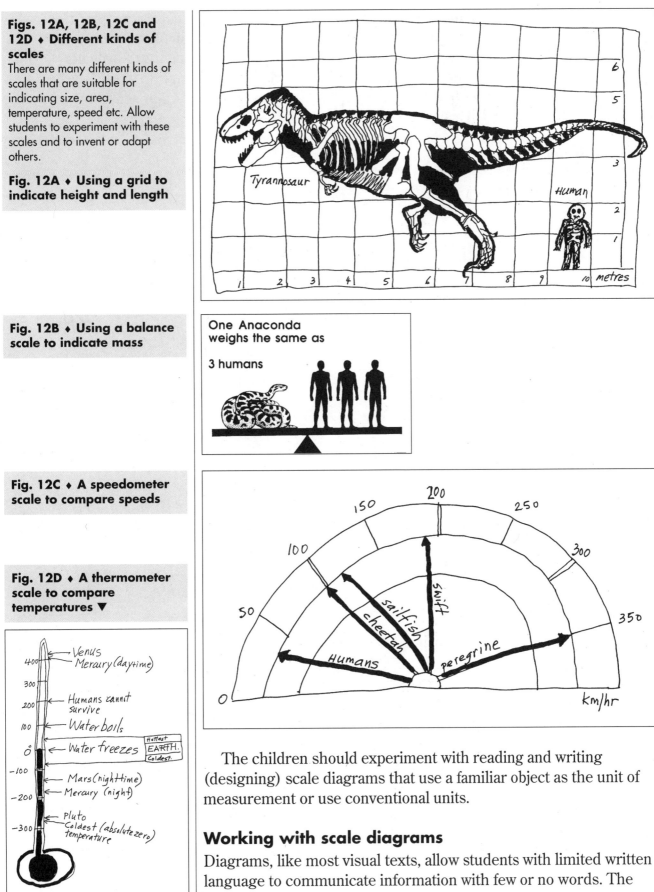

**Fig. 12B ♦ Using a balance
scale to indicate mass**

**Fig. 12C ♦ A speedometer
scale to compare speeds**

**Fig. 12D ♦ A thermometer
scale to compare
temperatures ▼**

The children should experiment with reading and writing
(designing) scale diagrams that use a familiar object as the unit of
measurement or use conventional units.

Working with scale diagrams

Diagrams, like most visual texts, allow students with limited written
language to communicate information with few or no words. The

scale diagram "Brachiosaurus" (Fig. 13) by Luke, for example, uses words only for the heading. The scale is drawn in picture units (the windows of a high rise building) which require neither words nor numbers to make their meaning clear. Luke, who is in grade 2, was described by his teacher as "a virtual non-reader, non-writer but a good artist" at the time he made this text.

Fig. 13 ♦ "Brachiosaurus" by Luke (grade 2)
The scale is in the form of a high rise building and the units of measurement are the storeys of the building. This is an example of a scale made of picture units, in which no words are required to communicate the meaning.

Luke's teacher comments:

The children were put in groups of three — a competent reader, an average reader and a less able reader. Each group had a nonfiction book from which to read up on dinosaurs… The children read about a dinosaur of their choice looking for references to size. They then drew their own scale diagram. By working in mixed ability groups, more capable children were able to read for the less capable who could then join in the discussion. Because information could largely be presented in pictorial form, the children with writing problems could achieve good results.

— Grade 2 teacher (HC)

The fact that Luke has produced a text without words does not make it a less valuable text or a failed text; wordless graphic texts can be found in textbooks, newspapers, on packaging and in the street. They are as meaningful and useful a form of communication as a verbal text such as, "A *Brachiosaurus* was taller than a four-storey building".

The more detailed diagram of Saturn by Sarah (Fig. 14) combines a picture unit with conventional units of measurement. The Earth is drawn to scale to indicate the relative size of the two planets and a scale is marked off in units of 10 000 km. These two ways of indicating scale do not repeat each other however. Each adds a different element to the text's meaning. The conventional units allow an accurate mathematical value to be calculated for the size of Saturn, though the actual number, being very large, is difficult to relate to our everyday experience. On the other hand, the picture unit showing the Earth in comparison to Saturn, though less mathematically exact, gives a relative value to the size of the Earth which students can verbalise as "Saturn is much bigger than Earth" or "Saturn's diameter is about nine times the Earth's diameter".

Fig. 14 ♦ "Saturn" by Sarah (grade 6)
Sarah has indicated the scale of this planet using both a picture unit (the Earth, drawn to the same scale) and a scale with conventional units of measurement, in which 1 cm is equal to 10 000 km.

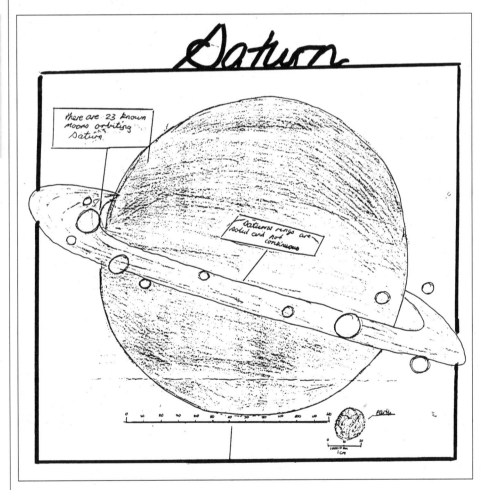

The asphalt chalkboard

Scale diagrams, like maps, are commonly used to reduce very large subjects (such as planets and dinosaurs) to the confines of a book. However, they are just as useful in making the tiny, even the microscopic, large enough to be examined and measured. Contexts for using these enlarged scale diagrams might include the study of items under a magnifying lens or microscope.

The same principles apply, whether the scale of the diagram is reduced or enlarged. Enlarged diagrams enable students to interact with subjects which otherwise are inaccessible because they are so small. For example, in teaching a unit on the human body, a giant diagram of the inner ear or of a human cell can be drawn on the asphalt playground, using a scale that allows the students to walk around and through the diagram.

Photographs and diagrams

Whereas photographs show us the surface texture and colour of a subject, simple diagrams allow students to interpret and reconstruct its characteristic features. In this respect photographs are often about an individual example's particularities, while a diagram makes generalisations that define or explain a "typical" representative. If simple diagrams are a listing and measuring of parts, analytic diagrams allow us to see the hidden elements of a subject. These analytic diagrams are discussed in the next chapter.

Chapter 4

Analytic diagrams

Analytic diagrams help us to see inside a subject and to understand the subject's internal workings by:
- peeling off or cutting away the outside layer (a cutaway diagram)
- taking a slice through it (a cross section).

A *cutaway diagram* (Fig. 1) helps us to interpret the relationships in three-dimensional space between parts of the subject. For example, we might use this kind of diagram to interpret the relationships between the working parts of a car or between the muscles and organs of an animal.

Fig. 1 ♦ Cutaway diagram
In a science unit on how gears work, an old pocket watch was examined after its back was removed, revealing its working parts. Students produced a number of different cutaway diagrams.

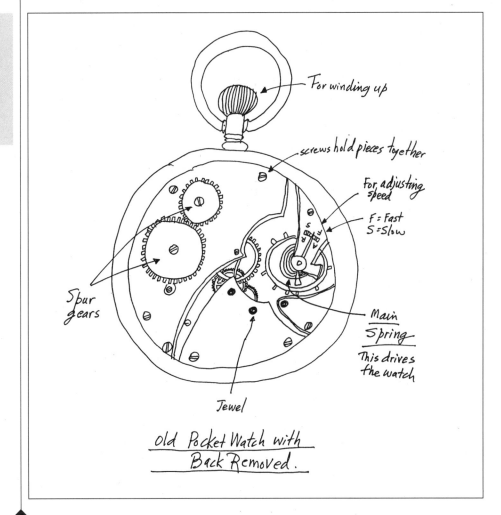

A *cross section* (Fig. 2) reveals the inside of its subject in one plane only, just as if we had taken a knife and cut the subject in half. This startling feat can be performed in a diagram, even if the subject is a germ, a volcano or a planet.

Fig. 2 ♦ Cross section of a cherry by Takashi (grade 5/6)
This student has drawn on both personal observation and book learning to produce this cross section. Takashi's text shows that students prefer to use the correct technical language if they are given access to it.

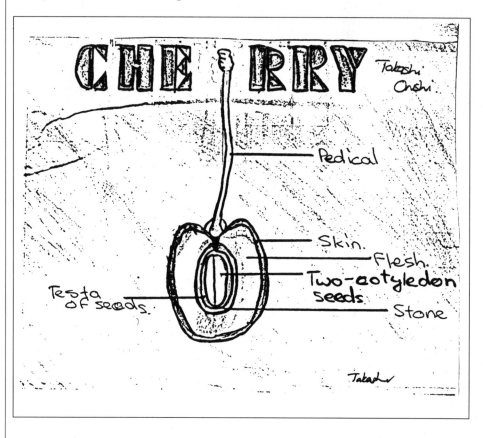

These diagrams enable the reader to imagine, reconstruct and analyse the interior of a subject that is either normally hidden from view (such as the organs of a mollusc) or can never be visited (such as the interior of the Earth).

Cutaways

Cutaways are visual texts that are typically found in books about plant and animal biology, the Earth and its processes, architecture and technology. They can be used to show and name the parts that are hidden or to reveal internal processes. Some cutaways, in manuals and instruction books, show us how to assemble instruments or machines.

Using cutaways

Purposes:
- to explore below the surface of a subject
- to show how to assemble parts of a subject
- to make connections between working parts in a sequence
- to expose and understand remote or inaccessible subjects.

Contexts:
- technology: engines, instruments and machines (such as rockets, cameras, pumps etc.)
- science: animal homes (such as burrows, warrens, hives, termite mounds etc.); plant biology (such as leaf structure, flower parts)
- society: pyramids, castles, skyscrapers; towns, cities
- health: human body.

Outcomes:
- can use a diagram to explain hidden processes
- understands that the subject has an internal structure as well as an external appearance
- interprets the diagram in discussion and by writing captions.

Examples in big books:
Alone in the Desert, p. 7 (making a fire).
The Cat on the Chimney, pp. 8, 15 (solving problems with simple technology).
What Should I Use?, p. 14 (gears inside a clock)
Body Maps, p. 13 (inner ear).
Rainforests of Australia, p. 26 (soil profile).
Natural Disasters, p. 6 (earthquake zone: block diagram).
Australia: an Ancient land, pp. 11, 14 (volcanoes and mountain building: block diagrams).

Examples on CD-ROM:
The Ultimate Human Body.

Introducing cutaways

You can introduce the concept of a cutaway by showing the students a simple model that allows us to remove part of its covering so that we can look inside it. For example:
- a doll's house or similar model, which has one wall removed
- a clockwork watch (or alarm clock) which has a back that can be removed to show the working parts

- a portable radio or cassette player with a back that can be removed
- an "ant farm" (or other animal nest) which has one glass wall for observations.

A doll's house

A doll's house is typically a cutaway model of a house, having one wall removed. Very young children can draw their first cutaway diagrams after first exploring a model house of this kind.

Older children can construct their own model house or streetscape in which one or more walls can be removed. Alternatively, students can use a piece of clear plastic cut to size, to make an "invisible wall". In working with these models the students should be encouraged to:

- draw and label the model showing both its outside walls and its internal parts (the rooms and furniture)
- design a "perfect house" by drawing a diagram of the house looking through the missing wall.

A number of children's toys also use the cutaway effect, such as toy cars whose doors can be opened or shut. These can also be manipulated, discussed and then used as the subject of a cutaway diagram.

A clockwork watch or alarm clock

Some clockwork wristwatches allow the back to be removed so that we can see (and repair) the working parts of the watch. This is the case with old-style "ticking" watches. Some modern battery-driven watches feature a clear plastic case on the front which allows you to see the springs and spur gears working without opening the watch.

The same is true of old-style alarm clocks. The clock can be one that no longer works. Remove the back and allow the students to explore and name some of the "clockwork" parts, such as the mainspring and spur gears.

Finally, ask the students to draw the clock as if they had "peeled away" most of the back of it. Have them label the parts inside. The result will be a collection of cutaway diagrams (as in Fig. 1, p. 37).

A portable radio or cassette player

Older students can study the organisation and working of familiar items such as a cassette player or portable radio, by unscrewing and removing the back of the case and naming as many of the parts inside as they can. A reference book of the "How it works" kind or a teacher-made word bank would be useful to support this activity.

An "ant farm"

1 If you are keeping small animals in the classroom, such as ants or earthworms, which make a network of burrows in the soil, you may wish to arrange the nest as a cutaway model. This can be done by placing the soil with the ants between two sheets of glass about 1 cm apart. As the ants make burrows and storage chambers, some of these will be visible through the glass. An "ant farm" container is shown in Fig. 3. Ready-made, commercial "ant farms" which resemble this arrangement are sold in pet shops.

Fig. 3 ♦ Introducing cutaway diagrams: an "ant farm"
Introduce the concept of a cutaway diagram by bringing into the classroom a cutaway model, such as an "ant farm".

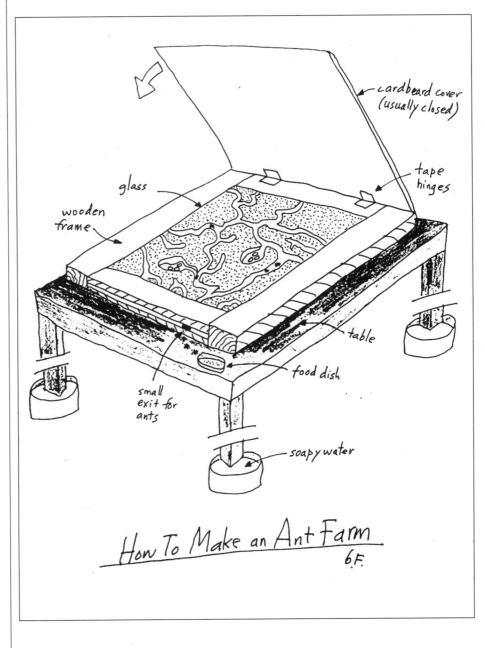

cardboard cover (usually closed)

tape hinges

glass

wooden frame

table

food dish

small exit for ants

soapy water

How To Make an Ant Farm
6.F.

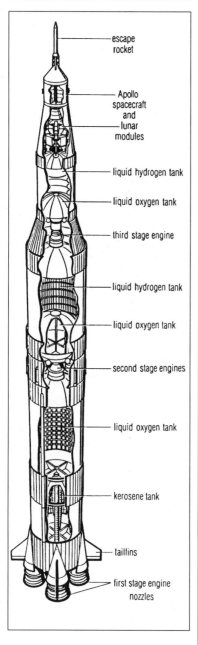

- escape rocket
- Apollo spacecraft and lunar modules
- liquid hydrogen tank
- liquid oxygen tank
- third stage engine
- liquid hydrogen tank
- liquid oxygen tank
- second stage engines
- liquid oxygen tank
- kerosene tank
- tailfins
- first stage engine nozzles

2 For most of the time the glass surface of the "farm" should be covered with black cardboard, so that the ants can go about their work undisturbed. Occasionally, you can remove this cardboard cover for short periods of time to allow the students to observe the colony of ants.

3 Ask the students to record what they can see when the cardboard is removed by using a cutaway diagram. Show them a number of different examples of cutaways in books, so that they can consider the possibilities of this kind of text. It is more helpful to show them a cutaway diagram of something *other than* the ant farm they will be drawing. By doing this they need to comprehend and apply the concept of a cutaway to a new subject and the children are not tempted to fall into the trap of merely copying one diagram into another.

4 You could, for example, show the students a cutaway of something as unrelated to ants as the Saturn V rocket (Fig. 4). Tell the students that they will apply this way of drawing to the ant farm. Allow them to make the connections between the diagram in Fig. 4 and their ant farm, which with its glass cover is a kind of three-dimensional model of a cutaway diagram.
Let the students observe and take notes of features such as:
- the way the outer "shell" of the rocket has been peeled away
- the use of labels to identify details
- the illusion of seeing inside and outside the rocket at the same time.

5 Applying this technique, students work in small groups to observe and record the ant farm using cutaway diagrams with labels. These labels may include questions, "What is this called?" as well as answers — "larval chamber", "queen" etc. The students may wish to divide the tasks among different members of the group. For example:
- two or three observers: using lenses
- a scribe: who records what the observers have noticed and the questions they cannot answer
- one or more artists: who work on the cutaway diagram (these artists can be the same people as the observers)
- one or two researchers: who are given the unanswered questions and who research the subject in the library
- an editorial team: who combine the information from the observers, artists and researchers and who offer a revised draft to the group for comment, correction and approval.

6 Finally, show the students some examples of published cutaway diagrams of ant farms (or similar subjects, such as bee hives, rabbit warrens, wombat holes etc.) for comparison with their own work. Reading other examples of the same kind of text supports the students' writing; that is:

- the students will be in a position to critically assess the published examples after having attempted their own
- seeing published examples will help them to compare and improve their own diagrams.

Make a list or table of what the students discover, in an open whole-class discussion, when they compare their own work with published examples, such as those listed on page 39.

Cross sections

A cross section reveals the inside of its subject in one plane only, just as if we had taken a knife and cut the subject in half. By making a cross section we create a new, two-dimensional surface on which we can represent its internal structure.

Using cross sections

Purposes:
- to investigate items that can be cut open for observation
- to devise diagrams that apply this principle to subjects we cannot physically cut open
- to write verbal texts using cross sections as sources.

Contexts:
- science: processes in plants, animals, the human body, cells
- space: Earth and other planets, moons, stars, imagined worlds
- society: underground energy sources, products and services
- health: food plants that produce fruit and seeds.

Outcomes:
- understands the differences between the internal and external appearances of a subject
- uses labelling and captions to support a diagram
- can construct a diagram from verbal information.

Examples in big books:
Earth in Danger, p. 15 (ozone layer).
Small Worlds, p. 13 (section of the planet Mars).
Body Maps, pp. 10–11 (skin).
The Gas Giants, p. 9 (planet Neptune) pp. 12–13 (moons).
Alone in the Desert, p. 4 (finding water in the desert).
The Cat on the Chimney, p. 6 (solving problems with simple technology).
Animal Shelters, pp. 10–11 (animal burrows).
Earthworms, pp. 18–19 (internal organs of an earthworm).
Natural Disasters, p. 5 (volcano).

Examples on CD-ROM:
Stephen Biesty's Incredible Cross Sections: Stowaway!

Introducing cross sections

Students can explore the possibilities of this form of information by:

- actually making their own cross sections (for example, cutting into and examining items such as plants)
- using cross sections in books as an information source, in which case they can recompose the diagram's information in the form of a verbal text (such as using a cross section of a volcano to write an explanation of how volcanoes work).

Making actual cross sections

To help students understand the principle of cross sections, arrange for them to cut open actual items such as fruit, and to draw and label what they find inside.

1 Establish the purpose and topic area first:
- Grow plants that make seeds, with the longer-term goal of removing and planting the seeds to produce a second generation of plants. You might choose to grow plants from packet seeds or from the fruit or vegetables themselves purchased at a fruit shop.
- Make actual cross sections of various kinds of fruit or vegetables, so as to inspect them with a magnifying lens and to record observations by drawing cross sections. Many kinds of fruit or vegetables are suitable for this activity, such as pumpkins, tomatoes, apples, carrots, oranges, celery etc.

2 Ask the students to form small groups in which they can:
- discuss what they can see
- draw cross sections, first without and then with the aid of a magnifying lens
- make lists of what questions they need to answer (for example, the names of the parts of the fruit) by referring to books in the library
- design graphs or tables with headings such as shape, size, colour and number of seeds in each specimen
- design a key to explain the parts of the diagram
- write a caption and heading for the diagram.

Working with cross sections

In a grade 1 classroom this strategy produced a collection of diagrams that showed careful observation. Haley's labelled diagram of an apple (Fig. 5) for example, notes the incidental features such as bruises, as well as the structural features such as seeds, flesh and skin.

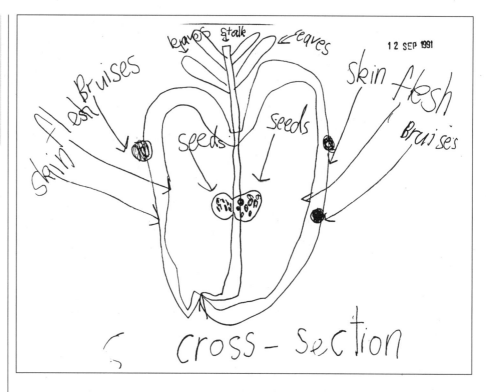

Similarly, Luke's diagram (Fig. 6) includes a speculation based on his observation ("holes made by bugs") and adds the suspected cause as an element in the diagram. This activity was done without reference to books; the students relied only on their own experience and close observation.

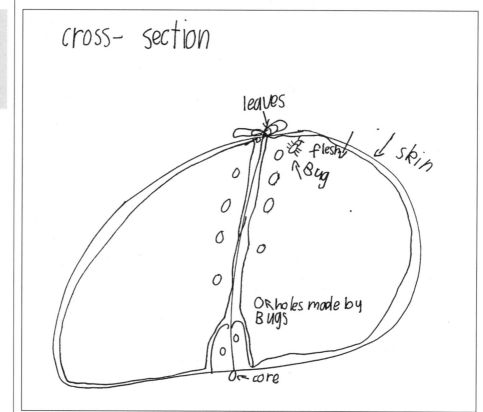

In the case of Takashi's cross section of a cherry, however, the student has referred to books on the topic as well as an actual specimen (Fig. 2, p. 38). Takashi's text refers to the fruit's "pedicel" and the "two-cotyledon seeds", showing a familiarity with (and a willingness to use) the correct technical terms for this subject.

Observing a plant process: water transport

Most plants draw water up their stems through narrow tubes called vascular bundles. The students can observe this process in the classroom and keep records of the time it takes, as well as making a cross section diagram of their observations, by following these steps:

- Cut a piece of fresh celery (about 10 cm long) and place it in a jar of water. The water should be about 5 cm deep.
- Add a few drops of red food colouring to the water. Note the time.
- Observe the celery at half-hour intervals until the top of the celery shows small pink spots. These are the vascular bundles.
- Observe the celery at regular intervals as the spots gradually turn a deeper red. Why are they changing colour? How long did this change take?
- Use a magnifying lens to observe and draw the cross section at the top of the celery.
- Find out the names of the details in your cross section.
- Make a list of information to accompany the cross section, explaining how long it takes for celery to draw water through 10 cm of its stalk. At what speed does the water travel? How often will celery standing 30 cm tall replace its water supply in a week? etc.

Using a cross section as an information source

Give the students the opportunity to examine cross sections in books and to write down as much information as they can simply by interpreting the diagram carefully.

Topics where cross sections are succinct and concentrated sources of information include:

- familiar objects that can be opened and studied, such as plants
- volcanoes, oceans, fossil layers, the Earth's crust and the cores of other planets
- tiny structures in plants and animals revealed under a lens or microscope.

Cutaways and cross sections

Cutaways and cross sections are very similar. The difference might be summed up as: peeling off the surface of a three-dimensional subject (making a cutaway) and taking a slice through the subject to show a new, internal two-dimensional surface (making a cross section).

The two elements can be combined in the one diagram, as in Emanuela's diagram of the Earth in Fig. 7. In this case, most of the information is in the cross section, which consists of the left half of the globe in the diagram. The remaining half of the globe shows the outer layer of the Earth, without labels or other explanation.

Fig. 7 ♦ A combined cutaway and cross section: the Earth by Emanuela
The left side of the globe is a cross section, while the remaining half of the globe shows the outer surface of the Earth that gives the diagram its context. Emanuela (grade 6) has used this combination of cutaway and cross section to summarise her research on the structure of the Earth. Most of the information is presented as labels.

Crust, 6-70 km (4-44 miles) thick

Solid mantle approximately 2,900 km (1,80 miles) thick

molten outer core approximately 2,300 km (1,430 miles) thick

Solid inner core, approximately 1,200 km (750 miles) radius

by Emanuela

This combination of cross section and cutaway provides a context for the information shown in the labels. The labels are a summary of Emanuela's research on the structure of the Earth, presented not as "notes", or as a list of "points", but more informatively as a carefully constructed diagram, in which the organisation of the information in the rings of the Earth is as important as the measurements themselves. Many of the diagrams in books turn out to be combinations of two or more elements, such as Emanuela's. Students should be encouraged to combine elements from different kinds of diagrams. Mixing these elements allows for a more complex text.

Analytic and synthetic diagrams

Whereas analytic diagrams expose the hidden structure of a subject, another kind of diagram serves to make connections between separate and superficially unrelated subjects. These synthetic diagrams often explain sequences and processes or classify their subjects into groups and subgroups or construct a web of interrelationships between subjects. Analytic diagrams divide a whole into its parts; synthetic diagrams organise parts into a whole. The next chapter looks at some kinds of synthetic diagrams in more detail.

Chapter
5

Synthetic diagrams

Synthetic diagrams make connections between the parts of a sequence or subgroups within larger groups. Often arrows or numbers are used to make these connections. Synthetic diagrams can take a number of different forms, such as flow diagrams, tree diagrams or webs.

Flow diagrams

A flow diagram links its subjects with lines or arrows to show a process that moves through time (such as a life cycle) or space (such as the water cycle). Flow diagrams are useful for showing change, growth or development, or cause and effect.

Using flow diagrams

Purposes:
- to define, explain or summarise a process
- to present a set of instructions ("how to make/do/cook etc.")
- to show changes, or cause and effect, over time.

Contexts:
- science: natural processes (such as transfer of heat and states of matter), cycles in nature (such as the water cycle or life cycles), growing plants, Earth processes (mountain building, erosion)
- technology: systems, engines and processes (such as the electricity grid, levers and pulleys, combustion engine)
- society: how products and services come to us (for example, water supply, mail service), cyclical processes (how glass bottles are recycled), historical causes and effects.

Outcomes:
- can organise information in meaningful sequences using a flow diagram
- uses numbers or arrows to show directionality in a diagram
- can read a flow diagram and interpret its information as a verbal text.

Examples in big books:
Small Worlds, p. 8 (how craters are formed).
Body Maps, p. 8 (shark's teeth).
Animal Acrobats, p. 10 (how kingfishers catch their prey).
Tadpole Diary, p. 13 (frog life cycle).
Caterpillar Diary, p. 16 (moth life cycle).
Earth in Danger, p. 10 (global warming).
Toy Designer, pp. 4–13 (instructions for making toys).
Rainforests of Australia, p. 27 (rainforest cycle).
Five Trees, pp. 3 (greenhouse effect), 21 (soil erosion).
Keeping Silkworms, pp. 11–13 (collecting and using silk).
Animal Shelters, p. 7 (nest building).
Caterpillars, pp. 15 and 19 (moth life cycle: fold out).

Introducing flow diagrams

You can introduce students to flow diagrams by asking them to participate in constructing one as a group activity. The purpose of the activity could be to investigate a process, such as:
- a food chain
- an animal life cycle
- a telephone network
- how waste paper is recycled.

For example, the diagram in Fig. 1 was produced in answer to the question, "Where does my egg sandwich come from?". The procedure was:

1 The students brainstorm information which is written down by the teacher on a large sheet of paper which everyone can see:
- eggs come from chickens
- you mash the egg with mayonnaise

- you buy eggs, butter and bread at the supermarket
- you boil the egg first, then you peel it
- bread comes from wheat
- the flour is trucked from the mill to the bakery …

and so on.

The list is not yet organised in a sequence; rather points are written down in the order in which they are mentioned.

2 Students then make a sequence of symbols or pictures to represent each one of these stages, drawing each stage on a separate piece of paper. They may add labels or captions to each picture.

3 The symbol texts are then spread out on the floor and students discuss the best (most meaningful) sequence in which they can be arranged and move the pieces of paper to improve the sequence.

4 The sequence is then pasted on to a large sheet of cardboard.

5 The students can add arrows or numbers, to show the sequence. A flow diagram such as in Fig. 1 results from this activity. You can then use this text to discuss related issues such as farm animals, transportation, buying and selling, preparing healthy food etc.

A flow diagram of this sort works like a word bank; that is, to focus on key concepts and to provide students with a language resource when writing verbal texts on these topics, but has the added advantage of showing the relationships and the sequence of the steps in the process.

Fig. 1 ♦ Introducing flow diagrams
Each student participates in constructing a flow diagram by contributing one stage in a process, presented as a symbolic drawing. The students work together to decide where each drawing belongs in the sequence. In the case of "Where do egg sandwiches come from?" only the first step ("Part one: the Egg") has been completed here.

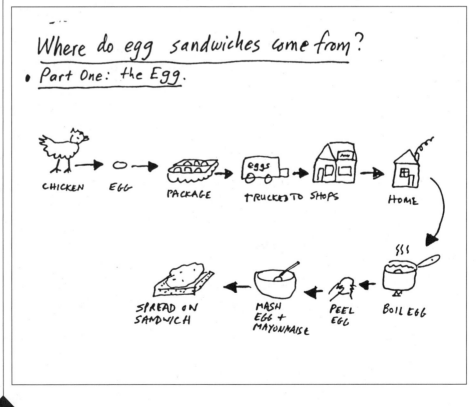

Summarising processes

Flow diagrams are suited to investigating or explaining processes, whether they are events in nature, technological processes or social changes. As a summary of interconnected events or causes with several results, a flow diagram can be a clearer and more concise record than several pages of verbal text. Areas for which flow diagrams are well suited include:

- processes involving heat, light, forces, melting/freezing
- photosynthesis, water cycle, life cycles
- products and services (such as where our electricity, power and water come from; the telephone system; recycling of materials)
- technological processes (such as how pulleys, levers and other simple machines work)
- historical change ("the discovery and development of...", "the spread of...", "the causes of...")
- origins (of the universe, of the motor car etc.) and extinctions (of dinosaurs etc.)
- Earth processes (such as mountain building, erosion and deposition, fossilisation).

Working with flow diagrams
Linear flow diagrams

The simplest flow diagram is a sequence of images joined with arrows. In Penina's diagram of a food chain (Fig. 2) the arrows indicate the left to right direction of the text as well as supplying the idea of nourishment, since arrows in a food chain indicate the direction in which the food supply is travelling. Several other details in the drawing add to this otherwise straightforward text. Penina has, for example, indicated the relative sizes of the animals, underscoring the discovery that animals usually increase in size as we move up through the food chain. Penina's teacher comments:

I used this strategy as part of my evaluation of a unit on spiders. I wanted to see how well the children could apply the information learned in the unit and present it in another form. I used the big book *Hidden Animals* (in the "Informazing" series) as a source and introduced the idea of food chains.

After some discussion, I asked the children to devise a food chain involving spiders. Some chose to draw and label, while others wanted to write and use arrows. I was surprised at the ease with which they picked up the concept of a food chain and applied their knowledge of spiders and other creatures to it. The strategy is well suited to young children.

— Grade 2 teacher (CW)

Fig. 2 ♦ "Food Chain" by Penina (grade 2)
This linear flow diagram shows the relative sizes of animals in the food chain as well as the direction of the food supply.

In the case of "How a Slice of Bread Ends Up As Toast" (Fig. 3) by Nenad (grade 5/6), the drawings are symbols which act as a visual shorthand for the words that accompany them. The captions in this text are more important than the symbolic pictures since the words supply most of the text's meaning. In the course of the text, Nenad moves from explanation (how "wheat is stored" is explained in the silo symbol) to instruction ("put in toaster and wait 1 min."), although the clarity and economy of the text does not suffer from this blending. As well as addressing us in these two ways, the writer also ushers us through the text ("this way ... down here ..."). These words act as a key explaining the function of the arrows. The boxed pictures isolate each stage in the process and they are linked by the arrows in a chain formation which moves down the page in a continuous zigzag. The sequence of boxes can be followed like a scriptwriter's storyboard, although this is not a narrative text.

Fig. 3 ♦ A chain sequence
The arrows link the pictures into a chain-like sequence. Nenad (grade 5/6) has produced a text which combines elements of a flow diagram, explanation, instructions and a scriptwriter's storyboard.

Forked sequences

More complex is Sarah's text (Fig. 4) which explains what happens to the water from the bathtub after you pull the plug. In this case, the text makes explicit the sequencing in the process (we follow the pipes like pathways) and this time there is more information in the drawing than in the words. The direction of the text is inferred in the visual idea of water flowing downhill; starting with the bathtub at the top left and finishing at one of three possible end points at the foot of the page (the incinerator, the fertiliser or the river).

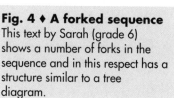

Fig. 4 ♦ A forked sequence
This text by Sarah (grade 6) shows a number of forks in the sequence and in this respect has a structure similar to a tree diagram.

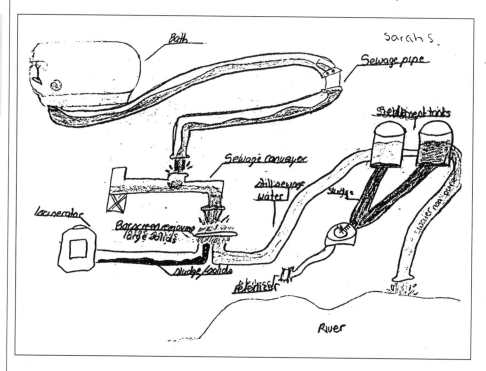

A feature of this text is the forking at three points in the sequence (the conveyor, the bar screen and the settlement tanks). This structure is similar to a tree diagram (see pages 60–64) where a trunk divides into branches. The reader is presented with a number of pathways through the text and is free to backtrack and retrace alternative pathways, as in a computer program or a choose-your-own-adventure text. Sarah's teacher comments:

> This task was set as a homework assignment ... The flow diagram was an important form for conveying information in the hands of those students who are having difficulty reading and writing (verbal texts).
>
> — Grade 5/6 teacher (BB)

Cyclical flow diagrams

Cyclical flow diagrams are best suited to describing continuous or renewable processes. Topics that lend themselves to these diagrams include natural processes (such as the carbon cycle, the water cycle or life cycles), repetitive processes in technology (such as how a four-stroke engine works) or environmental topics (such as recycling materials or feedback systems).

Yen's "Life cycle of the spider" (Fig. 5) recomposes information obtained in a book about spiders. Yen has employed two kinds of arrows, one large, the other small. The large arrows show the direction of the text and establish its cyclical structure, which has no favoured entry point; these arrows can also be interpreted to mean "grows (or) changes into...". The smaller arrows connect labels with pictures. The labels provide the minimum words necessary to support the information in the drawings, which show many significant details. For example, Yen has observed and recorded the correct number of eyes and legs and has also shown how this particular spider's legs are paired.

Fig. 5 ♦ A life cycle diagram by Yen (grade 2)
The large arrows establish the direction and structure of the text, while the small arrows link labels with the picture. There are many significant details in the drawing, such as the correct number of legs and eyes and the silk lines used by the spiderlings to "float" in the wind.

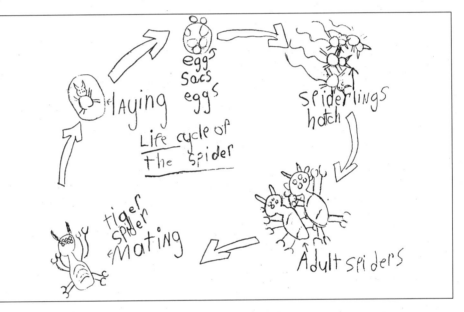

This kind of text can also be used as a comprehension activity, as a form of making notes and as a form of evaluation, as Yen's teacher comments:

I have a grade 2 class with a wide age and ability range. I used this strategy as part of my evaluation of a language/science unit on spiders. The Bookshelf title *An Introduction to Spiders* provided the information. The whole class discussed the events in the life cycle of the spider and the various stages were written on the board. The task was completed with a great deal of enthusiasm. I was particularly impressed with the children's concern for factual detail and accuracy, such as recording the silk line used by the spiderlings to fly off in the wind.

— Grade 2 teacher (CW)

A more complex diagram is Belinda's account of the water cycle (Fig. 6). At first the arrows appear to organise the cycle in a simple circular pattern; however, the hockey player's perspiration ("the moisture out of your body") is another source of water in addition to the ocean and this part of the text lies outside the main cycle. Belinda has arranged all the pictorial symbols (the stylised sun, clouds, raindrops, ocean waves or currents and the wisps of steam) in a meaningful sequence partly established by the arrows and partly by the direction of the rising steam and the falling raindrops.

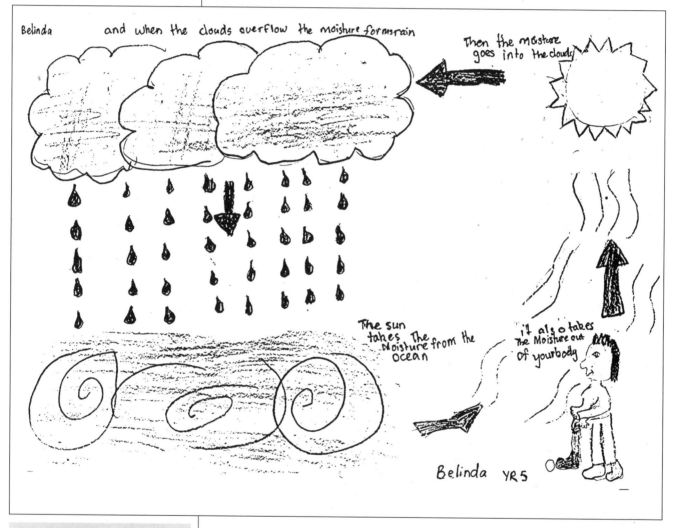

Fig. 6 ♦ Water cycle by Belinda (grade 5)
Belinda has organised the water cycle using symbols for sun, cloud, water and steam, as well as arrows and a parallel text in words.

We are given no picture clue as to where to start to read the pictorial part of this text; however, there is a parallel text positioned alongside the drawings, starting at the centre of the diagram with "The sun takes the moisture from the ocean..." and ending at the top left corner with "and when the clouds overflow the moisture forms rain". The words serve to interpret the symbol text, to provide a recommended start and finish and to offer the water cycle as a time sequence (with indicators such as "then ... and when ..."). Whereas the words treat the subject as a time sequence, it is the symbol text, organised with arrows and the implied earth-and-sky perspective, which provides us with the spatial organisation of the water cycle. In these ways the words and pictures make separate, overlapping and mutually reinforcing contributions to the meaning of the text.

"How to" sequences

Flow diagrams can be used to instruct as well as to inform. These "how to" diagrams, set out in a series of steps, are typically found in cookbooks, repair manuals, gardening books and in leaflets which tell you how to install or assemble your new video recorder, toy model or tent. There are many opportunities for this kind of text in the classroom. They may be produced either by the teacher or by the children or by both through negotiating the text. This kind of text includes:

- instructions:
    — raising seedlings
    — operating the projector
    — cooking pancakes
    — using the computer
- advice:
    — accessing information from a reference book
    — organising study time
- rules and agreements:
    — negotiating classroom rules and procedures.

Some of these texts can be displayed as wall posters.

Allow the students to discuss the pamphlets that come with construction kits or model-making sets. Some of these instructions are excellent examples of concise texts in which words and pictures work effectively as an integrated text; others, however, are difficult, clumsy and confusing. The students should have opportunities to become critical readers of information texts, to discuss how these texts could be improved and through these activities to gain a firmer grasp of the essential features of different kinds of text.

"How to" sequences can take the form of linear flow diagrams; they can be arranged as a sequence linked by arrows or organised by numbers into steps or stages. Another way to organise the sequence is to use a storyboard format.

Damien and Takashi (grade 5/6) have organised their text about making a paper aeroplane (Fig. 7) using numbers to indicate starting and finishing points and the directionality of the text. Although no key is given, we interpret the curved arrows in the drawings to mean "fold in this direction", while broken lines indicate the axis of the fold.

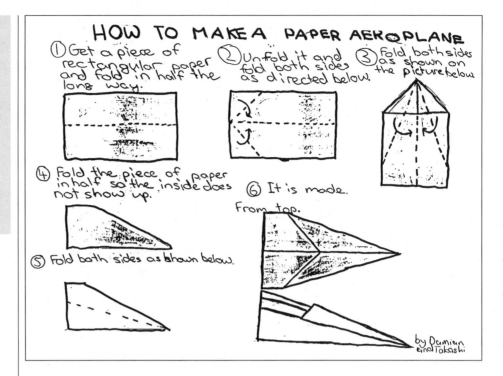

In the case of Marina's instructions on making a "Home made envelope" (Fig. 8) the text uses both directional arrows and a numbering system. There is a heading and a boxed inset with the subhead "Materials", which works like the "Ingredients" section of a recipe. The captions show a very exact and economical choice of words ("fold the paper in three even parts ... Put glue on the middle rectangle" etc.). The drawings support the words both to clarify and to add to the meaning. For example, the drawing shows the exact

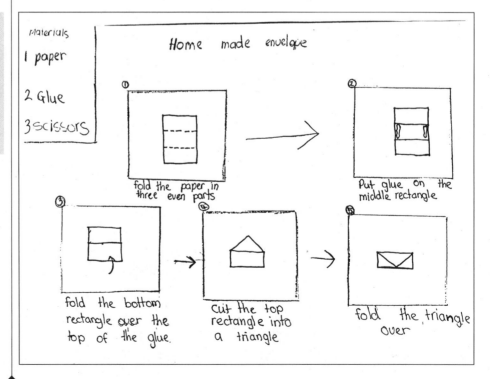

position within the middle rectangle where the glue should go. By putting each step inside its own box, Marina isolates it as a separate moment in a time sequence and frames it as a visual reference against which readers can check their own envelope making. As a set of clear instructions on how to make an envelope this text can hardly be improved.

Marina (grade 6) is in a K–6 classroom in a small, rural one-teacher school. This meant that everyone in the class regardless of grade level had the opportunity to attempt a "how to" sequence at the same time and younger children could observe the older students' work in progress as examples on which to model their own texts. Luke (grade 3) is in the same room and his text on how to make a fire (Fig. 9) benefited from this peer modelling.

Luke has produced a storyboard text the frames of which are to be read left to right and the rows of frames are read top down, as in a comic book. The test of such a text is whether we could make a fire by following the instructions and in this respect Luke's text is a success. The words and the imagery are kept to a minimum, yet everything in the text contributes to its practical purpose. Details in the drawing provide instructions that are not as fully explained in the captions, for example the arrangement of the "Criss-cross sticks" and the relative sizes of the dry grass, sticks and "Bigger sticks". Above all, Luke has thought through a practical sequence of events that make the successful use of his text possible and his confident, no-nonsense words and pictures indicate to the teacher that on the subject of making a fire Luke knows what he is talking about.

Fig. 9 ♦ An instructional storyboard by Luke (grade 3)
This text uses the conventions of a storyboard or comic strip to show the direction and the sequencing of the instructions.

Tree and web diagrams

Tree diagrams take the form of branching trees that connect objects or concepts in a series of forked branches. These texts are useful in organising how information can be classified into groups and subgroups or in showing how some subjects are derived or descended from others.

Webs are diagrams that show many interconnecting lines or arrows linking parts of the subject in a network of relationships. Webs are useful in showing connections and relationships among the many aspects of a topic.

Using trees and webs

Purposes:
- to show how information can be organised into groups or sets
- to show interrelationships between groups and subgroups
- to classify subjects in hierarchies.

Contexts:
- science: how animal and plant kingdoms are organised, evolution, origins of living things, extinctions
- technology: classification systems, libraries, data banks
- society: genealogies, family history, historical change.

Outcomes:
- can classify information into subgroups using a tree diagram
- uses numbers or arrows to show directionality in a diagram
- can read a tree or web and interpret its information as a verbal text
- can organise a plan of a writing task or a summary of a reading activity, using a web.

Examples in big books:
Millions of Years Ago, pp. 16–17 (evolutionary tree).

Introducing tree diagrams

Tree diagrams organise information in hierarchies, according to groups and subgroups; each group is linked to its subgroups with a line or arrow which forks at each subgroup. Tree diagrams are suited to such topics or tasks as:

- reporting on or explaining how animals, plants or other topics can be classified into groups and subgroups
- tracing patterns of evolution, growth and change, origins and extinctions
- genealogies, family histories, historical development
- organising information hierarchically, as in library catalogues or data banks
- organising hobby collections, such as minerals, fossils etc.
- directions to the reader, as in computer menus and guide books

- summarising verbal texts, when reading verbal texts such as explanations or reports
- planning and organising paragraphs, when preparing for verbal texts.

For example, in a unit on forms of transport:

1 In a whole class discussion make a list (using small pieces of paper, one for each symbol or word) of all the kinds of transportation the students can think of, without any attention at first to the groups in which they may belong:

bicycle	four wheel drive	yacht
helicopter	plane	train
oil tanker	submarine	sailboard

2 Ask the students, "Now, which other ones go with this... (for example, yacht)?". The students move the pieces of paper around on the floor, forming them into groups. Add labels (headings) for each group:

wind powered	*aircraft*	*sea vehicles*
sailboard	helicopter	submarine
yacht	plane	oil tanker

3 It soon becomes clear that some labels (such as "wind powered") are subheadings for groups that belong under other headings (such as "sea vehicles"). Move the subhead (with its group below) under its main heading and use different type styles. Explain to the students, "We can use CAPITALS for main headings and <u>underline</u> the subheadings".

SEA VEHICLES

<u>wind powered</u>	<u>propeller-driven</u>	<u>other</u>
yacht	ferry	hovercraft
sailboard	oil tanker	paddle steamer

4 Transfer this to a sheet of paper and draw in the connecting lines or arrows. Explain to the students, "The arrows show all the subheadings that belong under this heading".

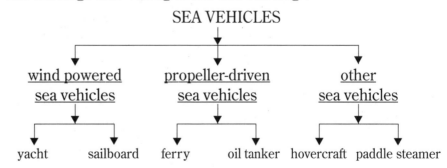

Explain that this diagram has arranged the information in hierarchies. The group *Sea Vehicles* at the top includes the subgroups below it that are joined by arrows.

5 You can develop this text by asking the students to:
- add further categories, using the same tree structure
- prepare a verbal text (a caption or a longer, paragraphed text) which explains in greater detail the similarities and differences summarised in the diagram
- the headings and subheadings become the themes of the paragraphs in the verbal text the students write to accompany the diagram: they can use these headings in their paragraphed text.

Working with tree diagrams

Nathaniel's tree diagram, "Electronic Media" (Fig. 10) organises categories within categories like the "Sea Vehicles". In a unit on media studies Nathaniel's teacher asked his students to explain where their chosen topic (such as radio) fitted within the broader topic of the media. In this elliptical text, we notice that at each level only one branch has been explicitly subdivided. It is assumed that other branches (alternative pathways) could have been chosen for similar subdivisions.

Fig. 10 ♦ "Electronic Media" by Nathaniel (grade 6)
Each row of Nathaniel's diagram divides into subgroups from one of the groups in the row above it. This kind of text is useful when putting a topic into its broader context or when organising the writer's thoughts in preparation for a verbal text such as a report or explanation.

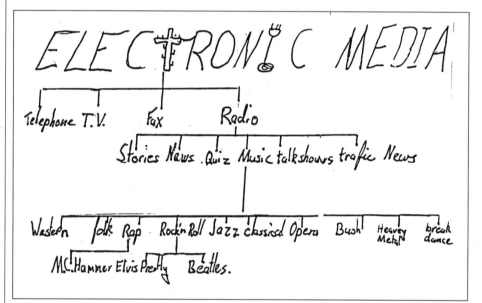

Maurizio's diagram for identifying plants (Fig. 11) was produced in a bilingual Italian-English classroom at the conclusion of a three-week unit on classifying plants. The purpose of this diagram is both to find the group to which a particular specimen belongs and to organise a hierarchy of plant groups. The text is structured to allow a number of alternative pathways to be taken by the reader, who is presented with clear choices and consequences. The author of this rather complex text is in a grade 2/3 classroom.

Fig. 11 ♦ "Flow Chart For Piante (plants)" by Maurizio (grade 2/3)

This tree diagram was produced in a bilingual classroom at the end of a three-week unit on classifying plants. The purpose of this diagram is to help the reader to identify and classify plant specimens. (*Ha radici?* Does it have roots? *Spore*, spores. *Semi*, seeds. *Felce*, fern. *Si*, yes. *E una pianta grande/piccola*, It is a large/small plant. *La pianta ha fiori?* Does the plant have flowers?)

Flow Chart (For Piante)

Maurizio's teacher comments:

I take this class for Italian half an hour a day. I do all my language teaching in a meaningful context: in this case we were studying natural history — plants. After six weeks of talking about animals and plants, including three weeks of classification of plants, we had just spent a lesson on what makes angiosperms (flowering plants) different from other plants; and another lesson on what makes plants without roots different.

Finally, we consolidated it all into a flow chart, to categorise a number of different plants. We brought pieces of moss into the room and we went out to the playground to look at larger plants such as trees.

— Italian language teacher, grade 2/3 (FK)

Tree diagrams and menus

Many tree diagrams are similar in structure to the menus used in the electronic media for accessing information, such as CD-ROM encyclopaedias or a search on the Internet. The user can choose from a set of options, each of which opens up a further set of options. This is an increasingly common and important aspect of accessing information and students are more likely to learn how to access a menu if they attempt to design one. One such activity is the plant classification system just mentioned; another would be to design and make a menu-style catalogue for all the books in the classroom's reading corner. A third activity might be to plan a plot-your-own adventure story in the form of a tree diagram.

Web diagrams

As cyclical diagrams or tree diagrams become more complex, we may choose to describe them as webs, particularly where we wish to summarise a process as an integrated network of relationships, rather than as a process that moves in only one direction. Webs are diagrams that link their subjects with a network of lines or arrows. Diagrams of this type include, for example:

- *food webs,* in which many species interact on many levels.
- *sociograms,* in which the actions and attitudes of individuals or groups combine to present a network of simultaneous interactions, attractions and conflicts etc.
- *concept maps,* in which ideas are shown to have many connections with each other.

Webs can be an effective form of organising ideas in many subject areas, including:

- history (multiple causes and effects)
- society (interdependence, conflicts, needs)
- science (Earth processes, states of matter, forces)
- technology (how machines or systems work)
- literature (character relationships and conflicts).

To take only one example, webs can be used to organise concepts and to find connections among concepts. For example, as preparation for a unit of study on the planet Jupiter, a grade 3 teacher handed out a sheet with some of the key concepts and topics in the paragraph they were about to read.

Some of the key words were placed randomly on the page as shown here:

```
                    planet              poison gas
        320 years              clouds                lightning
                    red spot
        crushed to death                  rings

                    Jupiter
                             16 moons
            total darkness
                    gases               volcanoes
                          giant
        hurricane                       dust and rocks
```

The students were then asked to make whatever meaningful connections they could by drawing arrows linking the words and adding any extra phrases that were necessary to explain the connection. One student's response is shown in Fig. 12.

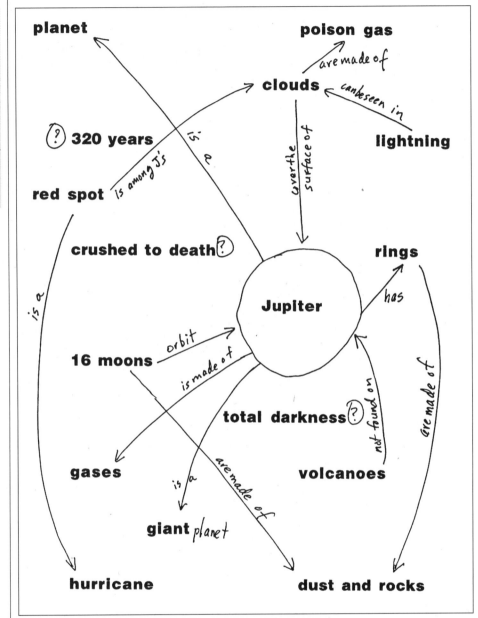

Here the student has formed sentences in which the arrows help us to read the direction of the sentence, for example, "rings are made of dust and rocks". Students were asked to indicate with a question mark any words or phrases they could not "fit into" the web. These queries acted as an incentive to read the text purposefully, as the students now had their own particular reasons to read.

The text they were then shown was the following:

The largest of the giant planets is Jupiter, which is made of the same poison gases as the Sun. Jupiter has at least sixteen moons and two almost invisible rings of dust, unlike Saturn's bright rings made of rocks as well as dust. Jupiter's surface is covered in clouds which are often lit up by lightning, but below these thick clouds there is total darkness. The atmosphere on Jupiter is so dense that we would be crushed to death by its weight. The planet's famous red spot, first observed 320 years ago, is a hurricane storm which has been raging for more than three centuries. Among Jupiter's moons are Ganymede, which appears to have moving continents, and Io, which has at least eight active volcanoes.

Diagrams and graphs

Some of the synthetic diagrams discussed here have relied on pictorial elements. On the other hand, tree diagrams and webs are often produced without any pictorial elements: they are made of words and arrows, in which the position of the words is a part of their meaning. In this respect, trees and webs show some similarities with graphs, tables and time lines. In these texts, positioning of the words serves a grammar-like function, making sense by linking up headings and subheadings with the words and phrases that belong under these headings. This is further discussed in the next chapter on graphs.

Chapter 6

Graphs

Graphs are similar to diagrams, since they are also texts in which the positions of the words (or numerals or symbols) are part of their meaning. However, graphs differ from diagrams in that, in general, they are less picture-like and more abstract and are concerned with quantifying (measuring) information.

In this section we look at two different kinds of graphs:
- bar and column graphs
- line graphs.

Designing and using graphs

Graphs are traditionally "taught" in mathematics lessons and are often studied as a kind of text which is peculiar to mathematics. However, graphs are as widely employed in books about science, technology, society etc., as are diagrams or maps. Graphs are a kind of text which has applications in all of the content areas of the curriculum.

In introducing graphs to students, allow them to design all aspects of the text. This means it is better to hand the students a blank page rather than a sheet of "graph paper".

1 You can use a graph to present information when you want to compare quantities. Don't make a blank graph sheet for them "to fill in". Let the children design the graph.

2 You can work on a graph over different time periods:
- in one session (what we ate yesterday)
- over a week, adding a little each day (weather details)
- over a longer period ("how many of our seedlings grew leaves?").

3 The graph can be made in different ways:
- on a large sheet of paper, scribed by the teacher during a class discussion in which everyone contributes
- different children add a piece of information each day to the one graph
- pairs or individuals make lists and later they compile them into one graph.

Bar and column graphs

Bar graphs and column graphs arrange information so that it can be:
- measured
- compared
- ranked (arranged in order of magnitude).

A *bar graph* measures information in units across the page from left to right (Fig. 1) while a *column graph* measures information in units up or down the page (Fig. 2). Otherwise they are the same kind of graph.

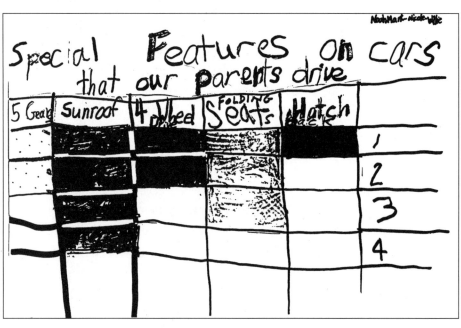

Fig. 1 uses a pictographic symbol of a person to signify each child-unit (or birthday). Fig. 2 uses the abstract, standardised area of each rectangle to represent a unit (presented in different colours in the original). Bar and column graphs usually have these text elements:
- label headings: to name the items to be counted
- number headings: to indicate measuring units along a scale
- rules (ruled lines): to separate the items in the graph and to link them with their particular headings and *either*
- cells (the rectangles in the graph formed by the ruled lines) *or*
- solid bars (the length of which represents a quantity on the number scale).

Using bar and column graphs

Purposes:
- to measure height, quantity, speed, temperature, age etc.
- to compare and rank information
- to summarise or highlight statistical information.

Contexts:
- science: weather observations
- English/language arts: book charts
- society: street surveys, opinion polls, voting, decision making
- personal development: behaviour choices (such as favourite foods, TV shows etc.)
- classroom organisation: activity rosters.

Outcomes:
- can interpret statistical information in the form of graphs
- understands the differences between rows and columns in a graph
- can link the information in the cells, row headings and column headings in a graph to make meaning.

Examples in big books:
Earth in Danger, p. 4 (temperature change).
What Did You Eat Today?, pp. 6, 7, 10, 11, 12–13, 14 (animal diets).

Introducing bar and column graphs

You can introduce young children to the concepts of a bar or column graph by using concrete materials such as counters, arranged in rows or columns. For example, a column graph can be built up as a record of a sorting and classifying activity:

1 Students bring one or two toys each to school and display them on a low table or on the carpet.
2 Ask the students to classify this collection of toys into different groups, according to categories which you can decide on together. Some possibilities include:
   - colour
   - size
   - material ("what are they made of?")
   - kind (vehicles, machines, games, model animals, dolls etc.).
3 Students arrange items in columns, count the items in each column and write labels for the columns, using a small piece of cardboard for each label. Show the students where the labels belong on the "graph".
4 Students write numbers (from zero to the number of toys in the longest column) to be placed along one side of the columns of toys, again using cardboard labels. Show them how to line up the number labels with the toys, perhaps using a long ruler.

5 While they are compiling their graph, ask students questions that require them to interpret the graph:
- How many animal toys are there?
- Which two columns have the same number of toys?
- Which are the most popular toys?

6 Students can complete this session by working in pairs to make their own record of this sorting activity by drawing their own column graphs.

Bar and column graphs are commonly used when making surveys. Students can conduct their own surveys and report their findings in the form of such a graph. Fig. 1 (page 68) was produced as a record of a classroom survey. The students were asked to raise their hands if their birthday fell in January (February, etc...). Each student recorded the results in a bar graph of their own design. Brooke and Belinda collaborated on Fig. 1, choosing to represent birthdays with "people symbols". This bar graph requires the reader to count up the units; other bar graphs provide a number scale across the top or bottom of the graph, allowing the writer to represent the information with solid bars that line up with one of the numbers.

To emphasise the measuring aspect of bar and column graphs the children can use strips of coloured paper to make their graphs. Using something as abstract as a square of colour to represent a person, a vehicle or some other item helps students to see that the graph deals with numerical values. The students can measure and cut the strips to the agreed length and paste them on the graph. Large-scale graphs can be made in this way for display on the wall as a model for students when they are working on their own smaller graphs.

Turning graphs into verbal text

In the case of the mail survey (Fig. 3), a kindergarten/grade 1 class kept a record of the mail that arrived at the school over a short period. Since this was not viewed simply as a mathematics activity, the students were expected to discuss and write about the information they learned from working on this text, which was treated as an information source just as any verbal text, map or diagram. Lachlan's interpretation of the graph (Fig. 4) is an example of recomposing.

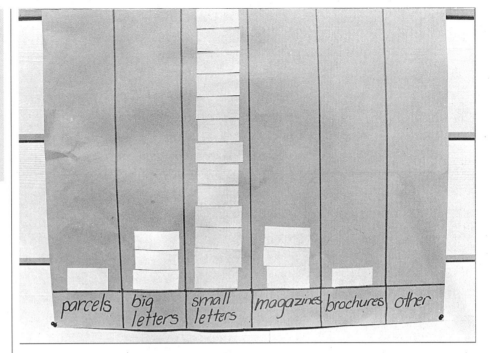

parcels | big letters | small letters | magazines | brochures | other

His teacher comments:

The children had looked at graphs and participated in making one shortly before this activity. They checked the mail each day, sorting it and placing coloured cards (one for each piece of mail) in columns that had been previously discussed and written on the graph.

After questions and discussion the children completed a piece of writing about the graph during a normal writing session.

— Kindergarten/grade 1 teacher (CP)

Fig. 4 ♦ Lachlan's interpretation of the mail graph
Lachlan (grade 1) was asked to write down some of the facts in the mail graph (Fig. 3).

One day we got all the letters and the most was small letters the Least was the brochures the Sekhd was the big letters and parcels and magazines ther was 27 small Letters and 6 others and we got m from the mail box.

Lachlan

Graphs can yield many facts, depending on the questions we ask of the text. For example, in the case of Fig. 1 (page 68), you could ask the children:

- Does our class have as many birthdays in autumn as it has in spring?
- In which three-month period will we have only four birthdays?

Working with bar and column graphs
The book chart
Bar and column graphs are useful ways of recording survey results, as discussed already in the birthday graph (Fig. 1). Other survey topics include:

- a record of the minimum and maximum temperatures each day for a week or once a week over a year
- a graph of the most useful reference books on a given topic
- traffic surveys, opinion polls, recording voting patterns for school positions, making democratic decisions in the classroom
- survey preferences in the class, such as favourite foods, TV shows etc.

One kind of graph which has uses for both the students and the teacher is a bar graph which lists the books available in the classroom's book corner when working on a chosen topic.

As the students complete a book, they write their comments and their initials or name in one of the boxes, which should be large enough to fit several words. This chart (Fig. 5) has a number of uses:

- it lets you know which books (and which kinds of books) were most useful to the students
- it allows students to read what others have thought or found useful about the book and is an aid to selecting appropriate texts on the topic.

In this case, the statistical aspect of the graph is perhaps less important than the comments made by the students.

Fig. 5 ♦ The book chart
This bar graph was used to record which books were the most widely used during a dinosaur theme. The chart also provided an opportunity for students to comment on the books' usefulness.

BOOKS \ READERS' COMMENTS	1	2	3	4
DINOSAUR (Eyewitness Guide)	We looked at it for Teeth. Marc.	Good photos and captions. Melanie	Skeletons and tall BONES. Michael	
FOSSIL (Eyewitness Guide)	See P. 48. Fossil giants. Katie. Amy. H.	Explains how fossils are made.		
PREHISTORIC ATLAS				
THE NEW DINOSAURS by Dougal Dixon	imaginary dinosaurs BEN.			
THE STORY OF LIFE ON EARTH by Michael Benton	BEST for time LINES — Donna.	Good pictures and maps. LUKE.		
COLLINS GUIDE TO DINOSAURS	No color. But has diagrams. Scott.			
PREDATORY DINOSAURS by Gregory S. Paul	Too much writing. Marc and John.			

Line graphs

Whereas bar and column graphs compare different subjects, line graphs are typically used to show changes to the size or value of the same subject. Often line graphs represent development over time and are therefore especially useful in learning areas such as science, society and personal development.

Using line graphs

Purposes:
- to summarise processes, such as growth, development and change
- to show significant patterns, such as cause and effect or trends over time
- to simplify and clarify patterns of information consisting of a large amount of data
- to find relationships between patterns of information.

Contexts:
- science: gradual change (such as weather and climate patterns)
- society: changes in populations, technology, land use; voting patterns, changing opinions
- personal development: values, decision making, health and fitness testing.

Outcomes:
- can interpret labels, coordinate points etc., to construct meaning
- can hypothesise about relationships between different lines in a multiple line graph
- uses different kinds of graphs appropriately for different purposes.

Fig. 6A ♦ Sunrise and sunset over 12 months: arranged as a table
Sunrise and sunset on the first day of each month was recorded for a whole year, using an almanac as reference.

Month (first of)	Sunrise (a.m.)	Sunset (p.m.)
January	4 47	7 09
February	5 16	7 01
March	5 42	6 33
April	6 07	5 51
May	6 29	5 15
June	6 51	4 54
July	7 01	4 57
August	6 48	5 15
September	6 15	5 37
October	5 34	5 57
November	4 56	6 22
December	4 37	6 51

Line graphs are also suited to visualising hidden (or obscure) patterns among many tiny pieces of information. For example, the times of sunrise and sunset over twelve months, when recomposed in the form of a table (Fig. 6A), appear as random items of data without any obvious pattern, whereas the same information recomposed as a line graph (Fig. 6B) is shown to have a clear structure in the data. The line graph allows us to see immediately the trend towards shorter days until June and July are reached, after which the days become longer. (The times are for Sydney, Australia, where January is midsummer and July is midwinter.) Although the

Fig. 6B ♦ Daylight chart
The graph recomposes the information found in Fig. 6A and clearly shows the trend towards shorter days in midwinter.

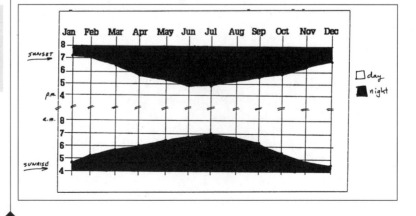

trend is there in the table, it is "hidden" in the data. Simply by plotting the data as a line graph we lift out this significant pattern from its background.

Some of the observations children can make on seeing such a graph as Fig. 6B, include:
- every month from February to June the sun sets earlier
- the days are getting shorter up to June, then after June they get longer
- the nights are about four hours longer than the days in June.

These observations can lead to speculations such as:
- Will the pattern be exactly the same next year?
- What causes this change in the hours of daylight?
- June and July have the shortest days of the year in the Southern Hemisphere. When are the shortest days in the Northern Hemisphere?

Introducing line graphs
Graphing with pins and wool

You can introduce the concept of line graphs for very young children using a pin board, pins and wool. The data could be recorded over a period of two or more weeks and topics might include:
- how much our pet mice eat each day
- noon temperatures as measured (1) near the window (2) near the heater (3) in the corridor
- a seedling box survey: height and number of leaves (Fig. 7)
- the number of bottles, paper scraps, cardboard packages etc., collected each week for recycling.

Fig. 7 ♦ Pin and wool graph: seedling height and number of leaves

The students can record changes in a plant's growth in the classroom by adding pins to the graph at an agreed time each week. This graph has two units of measurement: the left hand scale shows the number of leaves, while the right hand scale shows the height. Each horizontal line in the graph therefore has two meanings.

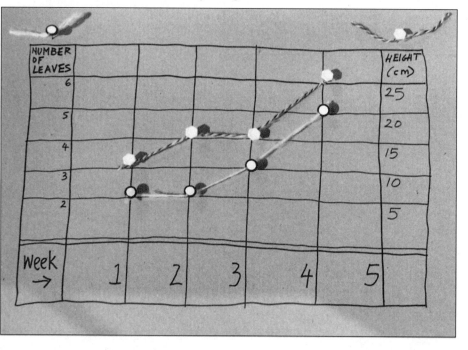

1 Allow the students to help design the graph, not just fill it in. Show the students examples of line graphs on other topics first.

2 Set up a large pin board on a wall at a comfortable height which allows the students to add information to it each day or each week.

3 Discuss the units of measurement to be used (such as "5, 10, 15…" cm in Fig. 7). Write these on a paper strip down the side of the pin board.

4 Discuss the times when counting and recording will be done (such as the date or "week 1, week 2 …" as in Fig. 7). Add these along the bottom of the pin board.

Before starting to record results, ask the students to predict how the graph may look in four weeks' time, by sketching on paper a line graph of their estimates.

5 Whenever a recording is made, the students should take turns in doing the counting or measuring and one child adds a pin to the board to record the result. Encourage students to interpret the meaning of the pin's position: "That shows it grew two more leaves this week".

6 When the graph is completed, help the students to join the pins with wool. Discuss trends: "This week our plant grew more leaves" or "The plant grew 5 cm in the second week, but it did not make any new leaves" (see Fig. 7).

7 The students compare the results with their predictions and offer explanations for some of the differences. They prepare a caption for their graph.

8 Ask the students what other changes or patterns they could record using a line graph. This helps children to identify the graph's usefulness.

Working with line graphs

The temperature survey

In a small rural classroom which included students from K to grade 6, the temperature graph in Fig. 8 was scribed by the teacher after individual graphs had been designed by the students. Before producing the graph, a pin board graph was used over a period of four weeks to record daily temperatures outside the room, near the window and near the heater. The graph shows the three temperature patterns for comparison, allowing students to generalise about the differences and to speculate on the reasons for some of the differences. In the pin board graph, the three locations were shown as differently coloured threads of cotton and these colours were transferred to the original written version of the map.

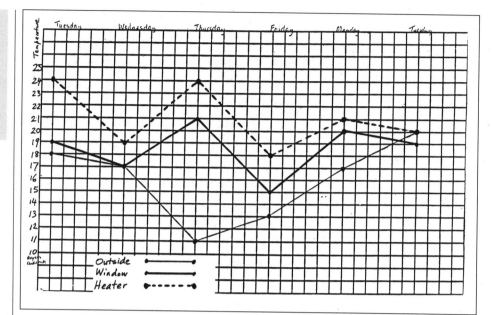

In this copy of the graph, instead of colours, the locations are represented as thin, thick and broken lines.

The teacher comments:

After the students had designed individual graphs, they decided on the format and made a class graph. We used a pin board, large sheets of squared paper, coloured cotton and thumb tacks.

The students were aware how much information had to be shown on the graph ... such as the temperature scale down the left side, the days across the top, the key showing colour coding of the lines (reproduced in Fig. 8 as thin, thick and broken lines).

Everyone took turns to record temperatures at lunch time...

Mostly the lines followed an almost parallel path, with outside temperatures the lowest, window temperatures in the middle and temperatures near the heater the highest. When this didn't happen (on the Thursday and the second Tuesday) I asked the students to suggest reasons why. Interestingly it was the younger (K–4) children who wanted to suggest reasons, while the older children (grades 5 and 6) were more inclined to say it was a mistake made in reading the thermometer or that the thermometer was wrong.

For the Thursday, Paul (grade 1) suggested, "We had to keep the room hot so that the cold couldn't push its way into the room, because it was a colder cold than the other days". (It was a day with an icy wind after snow in the morning.)

For the second Tuesday, David (grade 4) suggested that the outside temperature was warmer than the temperature near the window, "because the sun had come out on the playground but not on the window". (This window does not get any sun until very late in the afternoon.)

— K–6 teacher (one-classroom school) (DS)

The teacher's comments make clear that the value of these graphs is as much concerned with the hypotheses they invite as the statistical facts they contain. Graphing is not only a mathematical activity, since it has applications for writing, discussion, logical thinking, hypothesising and further research.

"Which graph should we use?"

Different kinds of graphs — column, line or pie — compose the same information with different (sometimes unintended) meanings. Choosing an inappropriate graphic text to express the data can have the effect of sometimes misleading or confusing the reader.

For example, in one grade 5 classroom, the students were discussing favourite TV programs and commercials as a whole-class activity. The data was scribed on a large sheet of paper by the teacher in the form of a simple bar graph, using labels and counting marks:

Program or commercial	Votes	Total
Decoré	/ / / / /	5
Coca Cola	/ / / / / / / /	8
Arnotts	/ /	2
Cadbury	/ /	2
Triple M (Etc.)	/	1
	...	...
Total		30

Fig. 9 ♦ Pie graph: Favourite TV shows and commercials
Following a whole-class discussion in which TV shows and commercials were discussed and voted on, Warren (grade 5) drew up a pie graph which showed the relative popularity of each TV show or commercial as a wedge of pie.

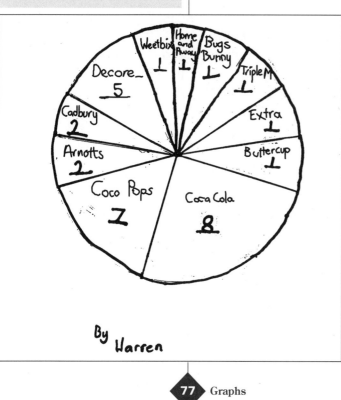

The students were then asked to design another kind of graph which recomposed this data. In Warren's pie graph of this information (Fig. 9) the data has been recomposed as wedges of pie.

Warren has performed some computations to get to this point, since the total number of preferences (30) divided by the degrees of the circle (360) needed to be multiplied by the "score" for each program. A protractor was then used to measure the units of the circle for each wedge of pie. The actual scores out of 30 were also added to the text as labels (such as "Coca Cola 8"); these labels work as a parallel expression in words and figures of the same data expressed graphically in the pie wedges.

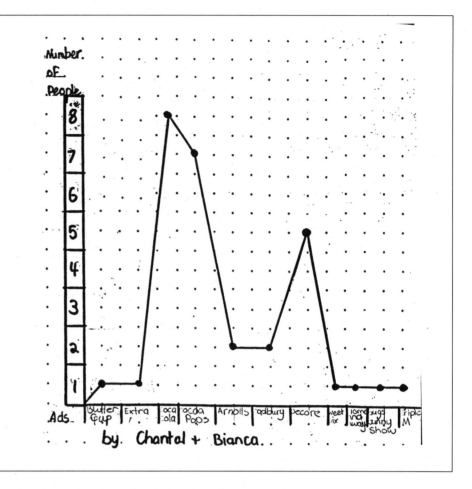

On the other hand, Chantal and Bianca chose to recompose the same information as a line graph (Fig. 10).

Whereas the intention of the text is clear, the continuous line that moves across the graph from left to right suggests a continuity through the data that does not exist. There is no actual process or sequence represented by this line. The information would have been presented without this misleading element if the line were replaced by a separate column for each label (as in Fig. 2, page 68), since there is no particular significance in the order in which these labels have been placed from left to right across the text.

Graphs, time lines, maps and tables

Graphs have certain similarities with other kinds of text such as time lines, maps and tables. Maps and tables share the graph's coordinate arrangement of information, using labels along the sides and top (or bottom) of the text; while time lines arrange events in chronological order as a line graph often does. In all of these texts we construct the meaning of an item inside the text by linking it with the labels along one or more sides of the text. The following chapters consider each one of these texts: firstly time lines and then maps and tables.

Chapter 7

Time lines

Time lines can be thought of as a kind of flow diagram or as a kind of graph. In the case of "flow" time lines, the steps in the sequence are joined by arrows, with little attention paid to the exact time period that has passed between each stage. In the case of "graph" time lines, the periods of time are measured in equal units along a scale, allowing the reader to calculate more exactly how much time has passed between different points along the line. In both cases, events are added to the line in the form of labels.

Using time lines

Purposes:
- to record a history or sequence of events
- to summarise facts in chronological order
- to summarise growth, change and development over time
- to find patterns and connections (such as cause and effect or recurring events) in a series or process.

Contexts:
- science: prehistoric times, life cycles and other natural processes
- society: changes in neighbourhood, local history, remembered events
- personal development: the students' lifetimes
- technology: historical development of transportation, communications etc.
- English/creative arts: authors' and artists' lifetimes and influences.

Outcomes:
- can organise data in a time sequence
- uses time lines to understand growth, change, recurring events, cause and effect
- can measure elapsed time between events on a time line
- understands and uses a variety of time units (minutes, days, seasons, centuries).

Examples in big books:
Millions of Years Ago, pp. 4–17 (prehistory time lines).
What Did You Eat Today?, pp. 6, 8 (one-week calendars).
Small Worlds, p. 14 (orbit of Pluto with dates).
Animal Acrobats, p. 10 (2–second time line).
Caterpillar Diary, p. 16 (clock face time line).
Keeping Silkworms, pp. 16–17 (silkworm life cycle).
Australia: an Ancient Land, p. 30 (prehistory time lines).

We can use time lines to help us both to summarise a sequence of events and to see a logic in these events. By organising events in their correct sequence we discover that they have meaningful connections such as:
- cause and effect
- each event builds on previous events (as in a history of flight)
- patterns in nature (such as melting and freezing)
- cyclical growth and development (such as life cycles)
- recurring patterns and correlations (such as seasonal changes).

Simple time lines

Most time lines are simply one-dimensional "arrows of time" that organise information in its chronological sequence. In the time line of a racoon (Fig. 1) the animal's day is summarised in pictures and words along a line that is read from left to right. The times ("6 a.m., 9 a.m.") tell us which way to read the graph, so that, although there is no arrow, the line does have direction.

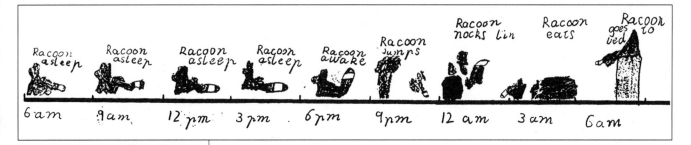

Fig. 1 ♦ Simple time line: a day in the life of a racoon
In this representation of 24 hours in the life of a racoon by Tom (grade 3) the time line is marked in equal units of 3 hours each. The time line is a summary of Tom's reading of a book depicting (among other things) what happens to a racoon in a day, for example, "nocks bin": knocks over rubbish bin.

Some of the information in Fig. 1 can be expressed as a time statement (such as "racoons are active for only twelve hours a day"). But not all the information in a time line can be expressed as a "number sentence". For example, by linking the behaviour of the racoon with the times it is awake, we can make inferences such as "racoons are nocturnal".

Multiple time lines

Time lines can have added meanings when we plot several subjects (several lifetimes, for example) along the same time axis, producing multiple time lines. These kinds of time lines are useful when tracing historical events which overlap and have a bearing on one another. Contexts for these multiple time lines might include:
- recent children's writers
- women in science
- the development of flight
- personal computers since the 1970s.

Multiple time lines are useful when we wish to highlight:
- the influence of one subject on another
- contemporary or simultaneous events
- growth and development
- cause and effect.

For example, in Fig. 2, the overlapping histories of different forms of transport help us to make observations and hypotheses, such as:
- for most of human history, the horse (mule etc.) was the only form of transportation
- there are more forms of aerial transport now than at any time in the past
- why were airships abandoned as passenger vehicles in 1937?

When showing students examples of time lines such as Fig. 2, it is helpful to draw attention to the text elements; for example, to point out:
- events that line up above any one date are contemporary (simultaneous)
- the time-break symbol (⌐√⌐) indicates a "missing" period of time
- the symbols in the text (such as the VFT or very fast train) represent only approximate dates when a form of transportation

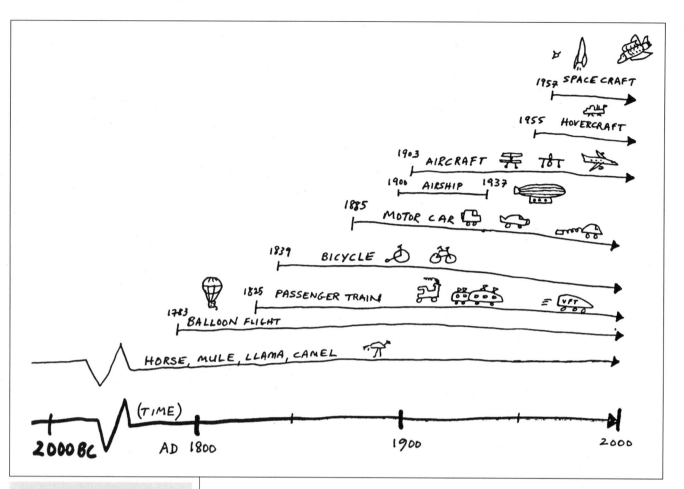

Fig. 2 ♦ A multiple time line: transport

Various forms of transport since 2000 BC are shown in this time line in such a way as to allow students to discuss and hypothesise; for example, they may ask how earlier inventions may have influenced later ones.

was invented or changed

- the lifetimes in this diagram are ranked in order (the oldest form of transport is at the bottom of the text, while the most recent is at the top)
- the text gives no indication of where (in which countries) these forms of transport may be found.

Introducing time lines

The concept of a time line can be established with the students using concrete materials such as string and cardboard labels ("a dinosaur time line") or computer paper ("a lifetime chart"):

A dinosaur time line

1 A string can be stretched along the ground with cardboard labels tied to the string at intervals of one metre: each label represents ten million years. The string will need to be 22 metres long in order to represent the period from the first dinosaurs until the present. The extinction of the dinosaurs is at 6·5 metres, while the first human is at 20 cm.

2 The students can investigate the times when various other dinosaurs lived; and they can make illustrated labels showing the dinosaur's name and time of first/last appearance. These illustrated labels can then be tied to the correct points along the string.

3 Take the string and labels out on to an open area such as the school playground, in order to show the students the relative distances (or times) indicated by the labels along the time line.

4 Students can use this experience as the basis for shorter (smaller scale) dinosaur time lines produced on paper in the classroom. These could represent the same information but on the scale of 1 cm = 10 million years.

A lifetime chart

1 Using continuous computer paper (each fold of which represents one year) ask the students to write or draw major events in their own lifetimes. They should mark each fold with an age number (such as "2") and a year number (such as "1986").

2 Some students may wish to illustrate each event on separate pieces of paper and cut them out, so that the events can be rearranged in the correct sequence and then pasted on to the time line.

3 Explain that the space between each fold represents one year (which can be subdivided into twelve months or four seasons). Direct the students to place each event within a given year at the correct position, by asking such questions as, "Did it happen at the start of the year (at the end, in the middle)? Was it in summer? Did you finish that in first term?" etc.

4 Encourage the students to write labels for each event and a caption to help the reader interpret the time line.

5 Finally, the illustrations can be pasted in order along the time line. Count off the years and show that each "page" of the computer strip equals one year. The children discuss the numerical meaning of the position of the pictures ("two years after I was born", "the year before I went to school" etc.). During this discussion add captions under the illustrations.

Working with time lines

Time lines can be used to organise information over any time scale, including:

- one day's events, such as a zoo visit
- one month's events, such as weather patterns
- a child's lifetime; or a summary of the memories of two or three generations in the child's family
- centuries: such as an outline history of a past civilisation.

Young children can work successfully with time lines. In Adam's time line of his visit to a zoo (Fig. 3), the time is marked off in rhythmic units like waves. In this first attempt Adam (age 5.11) successfully conveys the regular pattern of time passing and also understands how to combine picture and label to make meaning.

Fig. 3 ♦ Adam's visit to the zoo (age 5.11)
Adam has designed his own way of representing units of time, in the form of waves. His drawings are supported by captions which are lined up under each picture, for example, "kas" (camels).

Although this kindergarten/grade 1 class had not been introduced to formal measurement, the students decided on the wave pattern as a way of representing the passing of time. Adam's teacher comments:

> After looking over a limited number of time lines, the children were asked to make a time line of their trip to the zoo. The "pattern" line was an attempt to show regular periods without the use of rulers.
>
> The following discussion led to one first grader stating that "a straight line would be better" and that they would need to "make short gaps for short times and long gaps for long times".
>
> — Kindergarten/grade 1 Teacher (CP)

In another classroom, Sissi (grade 1) was first asked by her teacher to make a table of "long" and "short" events during her trip to an aquarium:

Long	Short
1 We got sorted out.	3 We had recess.
2 We went on the bus.	5 We sat there.
4 We went on the ferry.	

She then drew a time line of her trip (Fig. 4) on a strip of computer paper. The numbers 1 to 5 in the time line correspond to the numbers in the table. Although the time line has no units of measurement, Sissi has stretched out the pictures of "long" events (such as the bus trip), whereas events which seemed to pass quickly (such as "we sat there") were compressed. These distortions were deliberate attempts to convey varying periods of time.

Fig. 4 ♦ Sissi's time line: a trip to an aquarium (grade 1)
In this wordless text Sissi has conveyed approximate length of time periods by the length of the picture; for example, the long bus journey is shown as an unusually long bus.

Both Adam and Sissi have improvised their own graphic conventions. Children should be allowed to experiment with symbols and graphic relationships in this way; just as they should also be encouraged to compare their work with the conventions in published time lines and to take advantage of these conventions in their texts.

A more conventional time line by an older child is shown in Fig. 5. Here Matthew (grade 3) has organised his lifetime using approximately equal units of measurement. His lifetime is measured both by calendar year and by year-of-age. Matthew employs symbolic drawings and words (both labels and captions) which need to be read together to make sense of the time line.

Fig. 5 ♦ Matthew's lifetime
Matthew (grade 3) has organised his time line using boxes and vertical rules to measure equal units of one year. Calendar years are shown at the foot of the text, while his age is shown at the top.

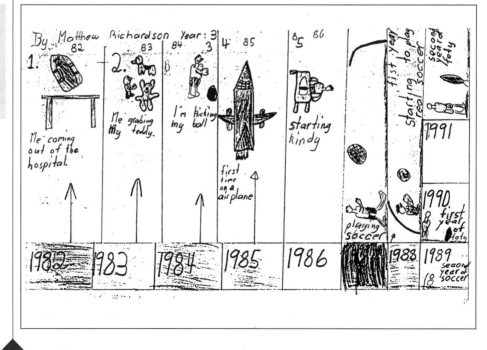

As Matthew produces his text, moving from left to right, he makes improvements to the conventions he employs. For example, while he uses arrows to link the year-label with its picture at first, he dispenses with these arrows in the second half of the time line, as they are redundant; the vertical lines of the boxes make a sufficient connection. Similarly his labels and captions show experimentation with different styles, ranging from the rather wordy narrative label "I'm kicking my ball", through to the more concise labels "starting kindy" and "playing soccer".

The directionality of the time line is altered because Matthew ran out of space; nevertheless he has the sequence right and he maintains the key conventions of equal units of time and concise labelling.

Time lines need not always be arranged in straight lines; some have more in common with flow diagrams. In the case of Kacey's time line (Fig. 6), for example, time flows — or meanders — down the page.

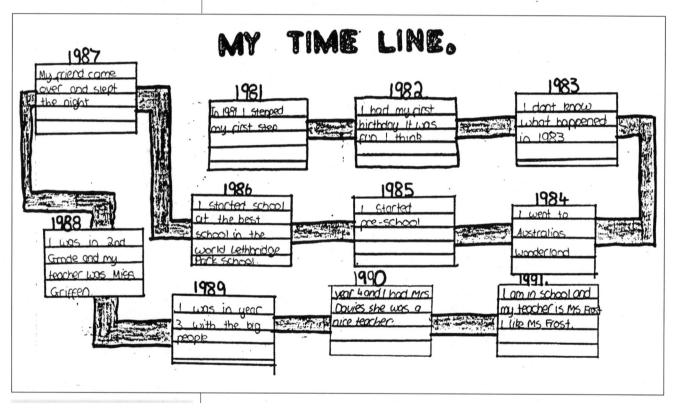

Fig. 6 ♦ "My Time Line" by Kacey

This meandering text by Kacey (grade 5) presents her life as a series of diary entries set in a river-like time line.

Its starting point is at first hard to find and the direction of the text is inferred from the year numbers alone. It is not possible to make any mathematical calculations based on the positions of the events along the time line, so it does not work like a graph. Instead the text can be read as a collection of loosely connected metaphors: time flows like a river, linking events which are highlighted in boxes that resemble pages from a book such as a diary, which in turn gives an appropriate visual context to the narrative or journal style of the writing.

Modelling the text

Students are more likely to produce a sustained, detailed and sophisticated text, if we model the reading and writing of a text for the students before asking them to write one of their own. This can be done by using big books (such as those listed on page 80):

- to show how we read a graphic text such as a time line
- to draw the students' attention to the text's key elements.

In the case of demonstrating how we use time lines and how they work as texts, we can interpret the time line in our own words and ask students such questions as:

- How long does it take for the caterpillar to become an adult?
- When did the last dinosaurs die out?
- Where do we look if we want to find out what happened a year ago?

In order to give students a model on which to base a time line of their own lifetimes, one grade 3 teacher produced an example for the students to use as a reference when writing their own texts (Fig. 7).

Fig. 7 ♦ A time line provided by the teacher as a model (grade 3 classroom)
The teacher produced this example of a time line based on an invented person, so that students could use the text as a model for their own time lines.

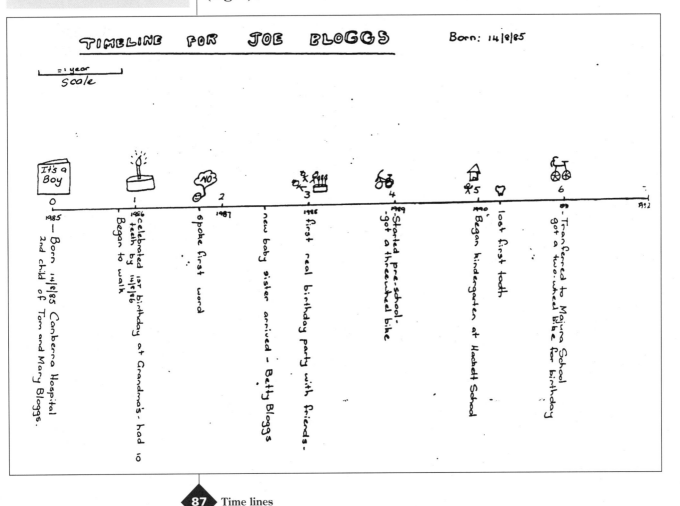

She explained the use of a scale (top left corner) and the significance of the positioning of each event. For example, placing an event halfway between "1988" and "1989" would indicate that the event occurred in the middle of the year or June/July 1988.

The students were also given a briefing sheet, which set out a sequenced task and which drew the students' attention to elements in the text such as equal time units, symbols, captions, a heading and a scale:

Make a time line to show your life so far.

1 Divide your time line into equal parts to show how long you've been around, for example, 8 years, 9 years.

2 Mark in the years, starting with your birth year, for example, 1985, 1986, 1987.

3 Write your age at each mark, for example, 0, 1, 2, …

4 Write important pieces of information about yourself along the time line, for example, "My favourite toy was …"

5 Draw pictures to represent some of the information …

6 Make a heading, for example, "Time line for Mary Jones, 1985–1992".

7. Make a scale to show how much of the time line represents a year.

I have put my friend's time line (Fig. 7) on the other side of this sheet for you to look at …

— Grade 3 teacher (BB)

The students produced the time line at home, where they could research their information with the support of a parent, to support their own recollections. An example of the students' work, which was produced using this strategy, appears in Chapter 2 "Reading and writing information" (Fig. 5 on page 10).

Time lines and maps

Time lines are suited to personal, local and world histories and can be adapted to subjects which cover a very short or very long time period. These texts, which help to place us in a time context, are often complemented in published books by maps, which place us in a spatial context. In both cases, young students are often helped to understand a topic by visualising it in the same context as themselves. In the next chapter we look at some of the ways in which maps provide a context for the student in relation to a topic.

Chapter 8

Maps

We use maps to place information in its spatial context and often to locate a subject in relation to ourselves. Maps are therefore not limited to studying "geography", but are suited to any learning area, including biology, astronomy, history, personal development and the environment. Maps can, for example, help us understand the weather, plan a vacation or follow the rules of basketball.

What do maps tell us?

Maps enable us to do one or more of these things:
- show spatial connections
- locate a subject and sometimes put it into the same context as the reader
- define territories (as in politics) or rules (as in a sport)
- summarise a process (such as migration, exploration or trade)
- show changes over time (as in weather maps, maps of ancient civilisations or maps of continental drift)
- record the movement, travel or spread of people, products or ideas
- instruct (as in a builder's plans).

In discussing maps it is worth remembering that maps can be of anything; we can draw a map of an ant's nest, a human tongue or a basketball court.

Examples in big books:
Body Maps, p. 12 (tongue).
Earth in Danger, pp. 6–7 (rising sea levels).
Small Worlds, p. 11 (radar map of Venus).
Somewhere in the Universe, pp. 8–9 (world map without labels).
The Book of Animal Records, pp. 14–15 (world map; animals).
Alone in the Desert, p. 8 (contour map with legend; map reading activity), pp. 10–11 (star map).
Looking at Maps.
Moving into Maps.
Australia: an Ancient Land, p. 7 (vegetation map).

In this section we look at three kinds of maps:
- bird's eye views
- context maps
- flow maps.

A *bird's eye view* is a map-like text that includes a number of different views, for example, directly overhead, viewed at an angle from overhead and a side view. Many young children's maps are bird's eye views.

A *context map* is a map of the child's immediate environment: home, classroom or the journey from home to school are examples. A context map shows the position of the writer (or the writer's place) in relation to other subjects; it can be drawn as a record of close observation of the writer's immediate surroundings or as a memory record.

Flow maps show a process or journey such as maps of bird migration routes, human exploration or trade routes.

Bird's eye views

A bird's eye view is an interpretation of the world which includes a mixture of perspectives; that is, directly overhead, viewed at an angle from overhead and a side view (what architects call an elevation). Young children's early attempts at maps are usually this mixed kind of text.

Using bird's eye views

Purposes:
- to understand the spatial relationships among the subjects around us
- to explain the pathways that we take
- to instruct others how to locate or arrive at a destination.

Contexts:
- society: community services, transport systems, communications; past civilisations, cities and countries
- science: mapping a classroom aquarium or "ant farm" etc.
- technology: designing a silkworm enclosure etc.
- personal development: the child's immediate world; that is, home, school, neighbourhood.

Outcomes:
- can explain and discuss symbols used in a bird's eye view
- can distinguish between a bird's eye view and a map view
- follows instructions in the form of a map
- can draw a bird's eye view of a familiar place, either by direct observation or from memory.

Examples in big books:
The Gas Giants, p. 15 (satellite photographs, overhead view).
Earth in Danger, pp. 8–9 (environmental problems), pp. 14–15 (map and bird's eye view of Antarctic ozone hole).
Somewhere in the Universe, pp. 12–13 (map view and bird's eye view compared, see also Fig. 2).
The Cat on the Chimney, p. 8 (problem solving situation using overhead bird's eye view).
Looking at Maps.
Moving into Maps.

Introducing bird's eye views

You can introduce bird's eye views by:
- comparing bird's eye views with maps of the same place
- making and discussing a model town on the classroom floor.

Comparing bird's eye views with maps

When asked to draw a map, young children often present us with a bird's eye view or a drawing which combines elements of both kinds of text, as in Nathan's drawing of his bedroom (Fig. 1).

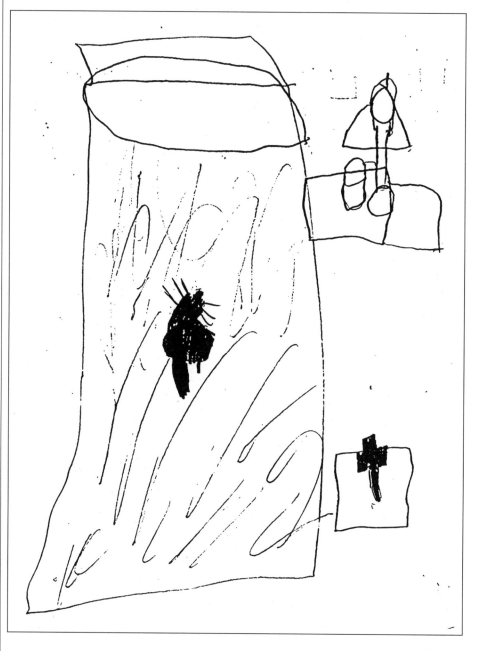

In this text the bed head is shown in an angled perspective, whereas the lamp on the bedside table is shown as a side view and the bed and table themselves are shown as they would be in a conventional map, without legs, as rectangles seen from directly overhead. Even the cat on the bed cover is seen in map view, whereas the glass on the table is not. The text is perfectly clear and meaningful and is not a "failed map". However, children should have the opportunity to notice some of these differences in viewpoint, as they learn to read and write maps.

When introducing bird's eye views and maps, it is helpful to share a map in a big book with the students, in order to explain and interpret the text elements (such as perspective, key or legend, colour coding). For example, Fig. 2 is reproduced from a big book which compares a bird's eye view with a map.

Fig. 2A ♦ (left) Bird's eye view

Fig. 2B ♦ (right) A map of the same location

In comparing the two, ask the children questions such as:
1 Why is there a bus in the bird's eye view but not in the map?
2 Why are the houses different colours (or shadings) in the bird's eye view but all the same colour (or shading) in the map?
3 Why is there playground equipment in the bird's eye view but not in the map?

In answering questions like these, encourage the children to make generalisations about maps. For example:
1 Maps don't include things which keep changing position, like the bus.
2 On a map colours have assigned meanings (defined in a key or legend) and in this map red means "house".
3 The third question may lead to a discussion of the different purposes and audiences of maps. A map of the same place, if drawn by children, could have included the playground

equipment in the picture. We could also draw a quite different map of the same place, if, for example, our purpose was to record only the neighbourhood's vegetation.

Making a model town

On the classroom floor define an area of about two metres square and explain that the students are going to build a model town in this space. You can define the perimeter of this area with masking tape, on which you can mark off distances, like a grid on a map, explaining (for example) that 50 cm represents 50 m; or you can use a tablecloth with a grid pattern as shown in Fig. 3.

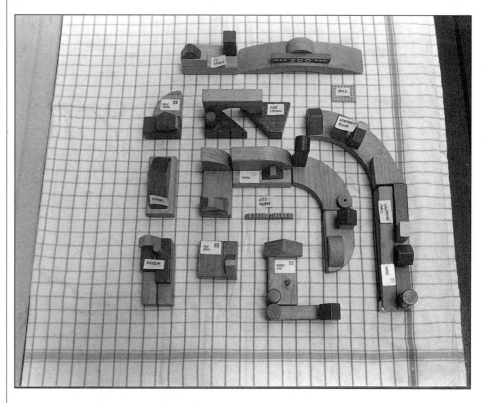

1 The students help you make a list of the things you might see in a town or city. This may be arranged as a table under headings such as:

Spaces	Buildings	Vehicles	Services	Texts
parks	shops	cars	lighting	stop sign
streets	bridge	bus	bus shelter	traffic lights
	offices			billboard
etc.				

2 Use wooden blocks, small cardboard boxes (such as recycled supermarket packaging, painted and labelled by the students) and toy vehicles. Include several streets. Encourage the children to make decisions about where each item should be placed. They

need to imagine walking around this city and using its services, spaces and buildings.

3 When the model town is complete, discuss the scale marked on the tape along the perimeter or the grid lines (as in Fig. 3) and if you wish divide the model into squares with string. Other items to add and discuss could include a compass (discuss the position of north and take a note of where shadows fall over the period of a day) and labels with the names of the spaces, buildings etc., that have been prepared by the students.

4 Discuss reasons for drawing a bird's eye view of the model town. Is it:
- to help people find their way
- to show only where the shops, parks etc., are
- to explain how to find someone or something
- to record every detail you can see?

The first three purposes will lead to selective interpretations of the model town; only the last purpose requires the child to "put everything in".

5 The students draw and label their own bird's eye views of the model town. They can draw this view from any angle or height they wish. You may need to limit the number working on this task to about four at a time. Since the students will be drawing standing up, it may help to use clipboards.

Display the children's bird's eye views at child's eye-height along a wall, so that the children can compare each other's texts.

Fig. 4 ♦ Mapping the model town
Ask the students to make a map of a model town such as in Fig. 3. Discuss what maps include and omit and how this is affected by the writer's purpose and by the map's intended audience.

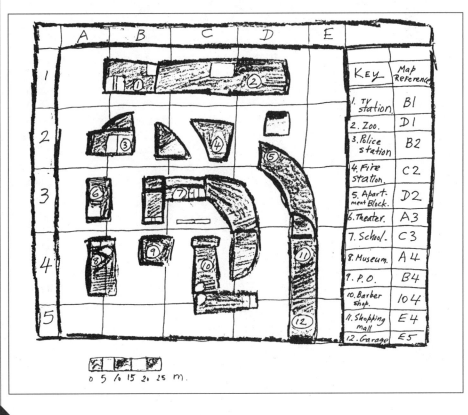

6 Take photographs of the model from several angles and display these next to the children's texts. Ask questions such as:
- What did we include and what did we (choose to) leave out?
- Does everything have to be in the bird's eye view, or not?

Comparing bird's eye views and maps

Some students may opt to draw a map of the model town, rather than a bird's eye view. All the students should therefore label their text "bird's eye view" or "map", so that they can compare the differences. Students who decide to draw maps will need to consider designing a key using the labels on the buildings etc.; they can also draw grid lines on the map which you may have included in the model town (Fig. 4).

Context maps

Using context maps
Purposes: • to help students to define and understand their immediate context • to represent the students' responses to their environment • to imagine and understand living in other contexts.
Contexts: • personal development: classroom, school, home, neighbourhood streets • society: shelter, community services, environmental values, other societies and cultures • science: homes for animals: the classroom's aquarium, "mouse house", rabbit hutch etc. • physical education: plans of a hockey field, basketball court etc.
Outcomes: • can explain familiar territories, pathways or activities using a map • understands the functions of a grid, key or legend, colour coding, etc. • uses a compass and tape measure (or ruler) to establish distance and direction before drawing a context map • can recompose information in a map as a verbal text.
Examples in big books: *Somewhere in the Universe*, p. 13 (street map with key). *The Cat on the Chimney*, pp. 4, 6, 8, 12 (maps which place the reader in context to solve a problem; maps compared with elevation views). *Looking at Maps.* *Moving into Maps.*

A context map is one which the students can draw from observing their immediate surroundings. The surroundings can be:
- the classroom itself
- home
- the journey from home to school.

The map could take the form of:

- a *jointly constructed map* in which the teacher draws a large-scale map, with the students' participation
- an *asphalt and chalk map* in which groups of students collaborate on a large-scale map on the school playground
- a *small-scale "pen-and-paper" map* drawn by pairs of students working together or by individuals working alone.

Introducing context maps

A jointly constructed map

You can introduce many of the concepts of map making, first by looking at large-scale maps together as a whole class (using maps in big books or posters) and then by designing a large-scale map, again as a whole class. You may choose to make the map on a large sheet of paper, on the floor or on the chalkboard, with the participation of the students. The reference for the map may be the model town just discussed, the school grounds and buildings or a large aerial photograph of the local neighbourhood.

The map need not be fully finished: the purpose of working together on this map is to introduce some of the text elements, which the students can then take over and use for themselves. These elements include:

- key or legend
- scale or grid
- colour coding
- compass bearing
- symbols (both conventional and invented)
- labels (both words and numerals).

You could ask the students to add items to the map on the board or to complete it as a pen-and-paper map of their own.

An asphalt and chalk map

Students can also experiment with map conventions on the playground surface, if you have an asphalt area that can be used for this purpose. The playground allows for large-scale mapping, in which the students can enter the world of the map, walk through it and consider the text from "inside" the map.

Pen-and-paper maps

Pairs of students can often support each other when working on small-scale maps. In this situation they can reinforce each other's recollections of the concepts established in the joint mapping session and can discuss decisions concerning details such as the units to be used in the scale or the symbols to adopt or invent in order to represent parts of the subject.

Encourage the students to use appropriate instruments, such as a straight edge to map streets or buildings, a ruler to make a scale and to check the size of elements on the map and a pair of compasses to draw door openings or trees.

Working with context maps

Classroom maps

For young children a good introduction to map making is to map something that everyone can see. The classroom is an obvious choice. The purpose of this activity is not to arrive at thirty identical maps: when displayed the maps are likely to differ and the differences will reveal information about the students' interests, values and attitudes to their learning environment, as well as their powers of observation and their skill in recording details.

The classroom map in Fig. 5 was produced by Lachlan and Adam, working as a pair, in a kindergarten/grade 1 classroom. The students have included a compass symbol (which is orientated accurately for this classroom) and an attempt at a scale: the "key" at the foot of the map which tells us that a plastic centimetre cube from a construction set (shown as a square) is equal to one hand span.

Fig. 5 ♦ A classroom map
Lachlan and Adam (K/grade 1) have included a compass symbol and a "Key" which indicates scale: one plastic cube (from a construction set) equals one hand span. The mapped items include a puppet show, a weighing station, a mailbox and two A-frame easels in the lower left corner.

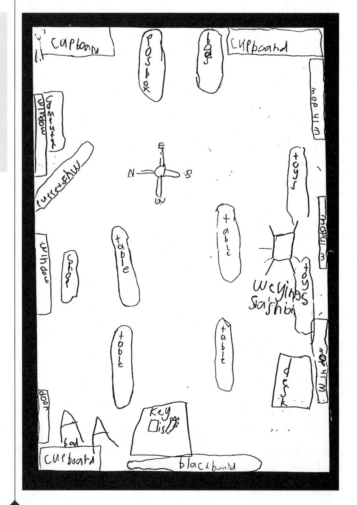

Accordingly, the students measured the blackboard with hand spans and converted this to a length on the map measured by moving and counting the plastic cubes. The sizes of other elements in the map are approximations. The walls of the room were not drawn in; instead, the edge of the paper represents the limits of the room. Some of the labels have been dictated to and scribed by the teacher, who helped the students get started by establishing the positions of some of the windows.

The teacher comments:

> The children were first shown maps and their attention drawn to relevant features. These included maps of the local area and enlarged aerial view maps, placed on the floor with children standing over them.
>
> The children worked in pairs to encourage discussion and problem solving. They had not been introduced to formal measurement, but had measured furniture in the room by hand span. The class discussed the idea of "scale" (for example, the toy shelf is nine hands long, but we can't fit nine hands on the page). They suggested the strategy of using one cube (from the classroom's construction set) as a measurement for furniture; however, the maps are not truly to scale.
>
> One student brought a compass in and the class determined directions to add to the map at follow-up time. Some children needed help with the labels and most would position themselves with their backs to the blackboard, to determine the position of things in the room.
>
> — Kindergarten/grade 1 teacher (CP)

Home maps

In another (kindergarten-only) classroom, the teacher asked the students to make a map of their bedroom. A number of the texts which this class produced showed a mixture of map and bird's eye view: one example was Nathan's bedroom (Fig 1, page 92).

The teacher first discussed with the students examples of map-like views ("we talked about being a bird or a giant looking through a glass roof") and commented that the students needed to see examples of maps before making their own:

> We drew a square on the floor representing the classroom and I showed the children where the doors were. Using foam shapes, I asked the children to place classroom furniture on the map.
>
> I then drew a very simple layout of my own bedroom as an example. The children needed this, before attempting their own bedroom maps.
>
> — Kindergarten teacher (RE)

Another child in the same class produced a drawing of her room and went on to make a map of her house (Fig. 6).

Fig. 6 ♦ "Lily's House"
Lily (kindergarten) has produced a detailed text which includes conventional symbols (for example, for the doors, the stove hot plates and the kitchen sink) and invented symbols (for example, for the TV set and the household pets). The rooms are (in counterclockwise order starting from top left): kitchen, living room, Lily's bedroom, hallway, parents' bedroom, father's study, bathroom and laundry. There is a verandah on the left.

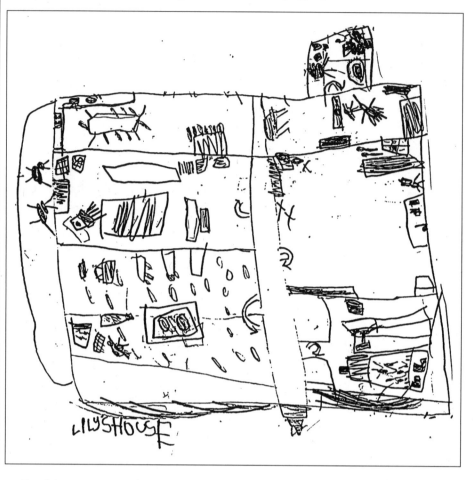

In this map of "Lily's House" we can identify the front door and steps at the foot of the page, the central hallway and individual rooms, such as the kitchen (with its sink, stove, table and chairs) in the top left corner. Lily has used conventional symbols for doorways (the curved arrows) and has invented others; she has used a mixture of top views (such as the kitchen stove) and side views (such as the pets on the verandah on the left). She has also invented symbols, such as the dining table and the TV, which are unmistakable. Lily's text shows a sophisticated organisation of details, including a great deal of information, without using any words except in the text's heading.

The students in a grade 6 class were asked to design the house they would like to live in. In this way they were able to tackle environmental and social values imaginatively, expressing them in the form of a conventional map. In Chris's house plan (Fig. 7A) a number of conventional symbols, as used in architects' plans, have been employed. Chris had worked on house plans in school the previous year and had seen builders' plans at home. In his "Leger"

(legend) or key (Fig. 7B), Chris provides us with the necessary vocabulary to decode his text. Most of these show correct usage of conventional building plan symbols, while others are his own invention.

Figs. 7A and 7B ♦ Chris's imaginary house
Chris (grade 6) was set the task of designing the perfect house. The students had already worked with building plans.

Fig. 7A ♦ Chris's map

Fig. 7B ♦ Chris's legend

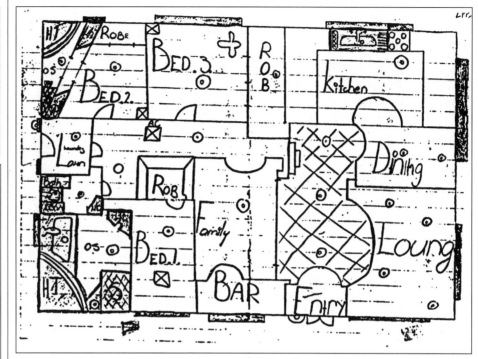

Home-to-school maps

Very young children's geography is at first limited to the world they experience between home and school; but they know and can articulate a great deal about this narrow world. Many young writers may not yet be able to put this knowledge into words, but they can articulate this information more successfully using pictorial symbols.

In order to communicate successfully using these texts, we need to give students clear demonstrations of the kind of text we want from them. One kindergarten teacher comments:

> As an impromptu follow-up to mapping bedrooms, we talked about maps and street directories. I drew a simple map of how I get to school and asked the children to give it a go. Again, surprising results. They could tell me about many features they noticed on the way.
>
> — Kindergarten teacher (RE)

One child in this teacher's classroom was Sean, whose home-to-school map is shown in Fig. 8. This economical text reveals that Sean has grasped many aspects of map making at his first attempt. He has drawn all the houses in the same shading, he uses a cross to indicate a Catholic school, the map perspective is correct and consistent, the streets are correctly orientated and the position of both "my house" and his friend Kieran's house are the correct number of houses from each corner.

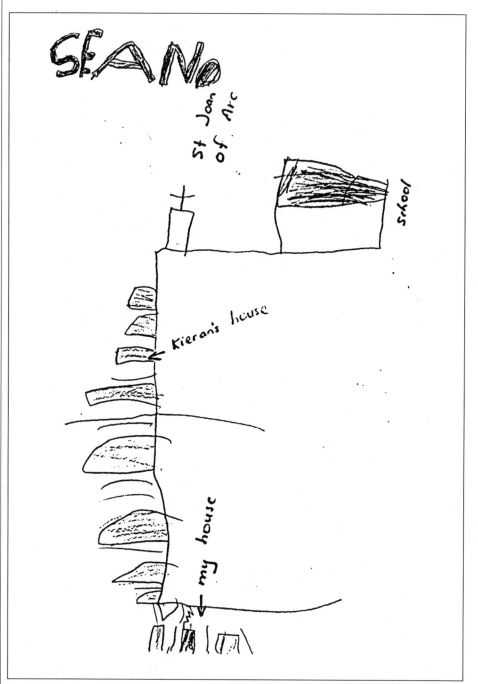

Sean has also devised his own ways to emphasise the important elements: the school is in a darker shading from the houses and his own house is the only one indicated with steps. The writer has conveyed all the information visually: the labels were added by the teacher later, acting as scribe on dictation from the map maker. As a set of clear instructions on how to get from the school to Sean's house, this text can hardly be improved.

Flow maps

Flow maps, like flow diagrams (see Chapter 5 "Synthetic diagrams", page 49), summarise a process that is shown to move through the space represented in the map. Maps of exploration routes and weather maps are examples.

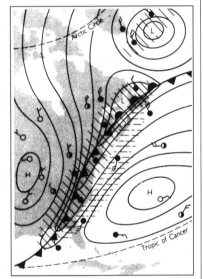

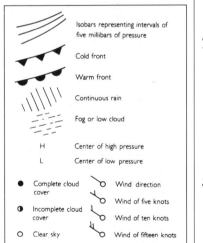

Using flow maps

Purposes:
- to record processes, change and movement
- to summarise journeys, trade routes, pathways.

Contexts:
- science: animal migration, weather reporting, Earth processes (such as lava flows, glaciers)
- society: human migration, trade, exploration, civilisations
- technology: local environmental changes (natural and constructed)
- personal development: what we do in a day.

Outcomes:
- can interpret the significance of arrows and other symbols on maps which show movement in time and space
- can record patterns of change using flow maps
- uses maps to support a paragraphed text and to summarise a text.

Examples in big books:
The Book of Animal Records, p. 8 (migration routes).

Introducing flow maps
Weather patterns
1 Ask the students to collect weather maps from newspapers. These can also be viewed as a sequence of maps if you choose to collect maps over a period of several successive days for comparison.
2 Like other maps, weather maps have a vocabulary of symbols which work to make weather statements about places on the map. Show the students a large version of a weather map such as Figs. 9A and 9B, which provides most of the standard meteorological symbols. Such maps are printed in the weather section of daily newspapers. You can enlarge one and project it with an overhead projector.
3 To introduce the idea of weather maps, ask the students to treat the map as a message in code. Using the key, they must write down as many true statements as they can about the weather. They may need to have beside them an atlas map of the same area, so that place names can be included.
4 Explain to the students that a weather map is a special kind of flow map: it shows a snapshot view of a continuing process, which

becomes meaningful when a sequence of weather maps are collected over the space of a week. But even if we look at only one weather map, a number of the symbols also imply direction and movement. For example:

- fronts move in the direction of the front markings; in the case of Fig. 9A the warm front is moving northwest, while the cold front is moving southeast
- the wind symbols indicate speed as well as direction; with this information students can make predictions about tomorrow's weather pattern by studying today's.

Not all newspapers follow these standard conventions in their weather maps. In the case of Fig. 10, the symbols for cloud, sunshine, rain etc., are provided in a form that almost eliminates the need for a key.

Fig. 10 ♦ Weather maps without a key
Many weather maps on TV or in newspapers do not use a key; instead they employ symbols which appear to be self-explanatory, such as those used here for rain, cloudy, partly cloudy and for the direction and speed of the wind. Placing a morning and afternoon map side by side invites comparisons and predictions.

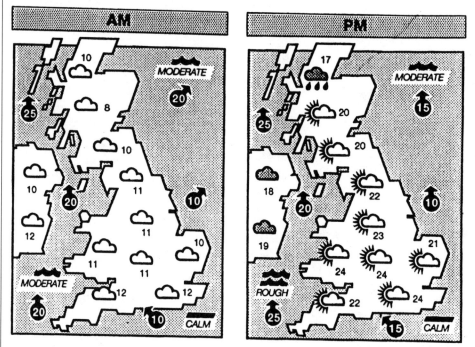

Children may like to compare how different newspapers (and TV weather presenters) have solved the problem of making weather symbols almost self-explanatory. The students may also wish to design their own symbols for use on their weather maps.

Migration, trade, exploration and other travel

The map in Fig. 11 shows the migration routes and overwintering sites of the North American wanderer butterfly, which despite its frailty and size travels up to 4 000 kilometres each year. This process is shown by the arrows.

Explain to the students that, whereas some of the symbols are explained in the key, others are left to the reader to interpret. For example, solid arrows seem to indicate proven flight paths, while

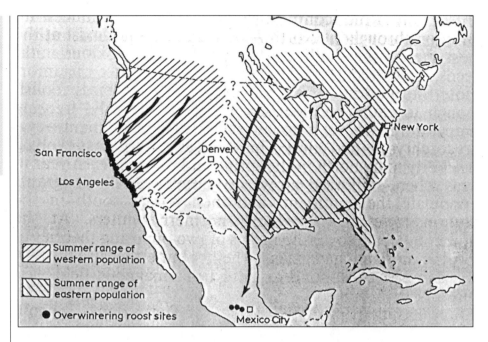

Fig. 11 ♦ A flow map: migration routes of the wanderer butterfly
The flight paths of this butterfly are shown by arrows. Some of the symbols, such as the shading, are defined in the key, whereas others are left to the reader to interpret, such as the broken arrows and the question marks.

broken arrows seem to indicate hypothetical flight paths; the question marks suggest a lack of data.

In sharing a map like this, discuss with the children how the data for the map might have been collected. Did people actually follow the butterflies or did they observe them at many separate places on the way, like the weather stations that phone in the air pressure results that are collated into the isobar patterns on a weather chart?

The students might also attempt to express in words the information conveyed by some of the map's symbols. For example:

- some wanderers travel from New York to Florida and may even cross the open sea to reach Cuba
- butterflies collected west of Mexico City are thought to have originated from Midwest USA.

The map also raises questions that can be answered only by further reading, such as, "How does a scientist in Mexico know where a butterfly has come from?".

Map coordinates

In demonstrating how maps work and how we use them, we can help students to access the data in a map more readily if we show them how the grid of a map works. We can do this by asking questions such as:

- The grid lines are all the same distance apart: can you use the scale to work out the distance between the grid lines?
- Here's our school and here's the shopping mall. Use the grid lines to estimate how far it would be to walk to the mall.
- On the top of the map the grid lines are numbered and on the side the lines are given letters A, B, C, ... Where they meet is the

coordinate point. Here's D6, for example. Can you find E10 on the map? What are the coordinates for our school?

Coordinates are a way of indexing the data on a map and allow us to find small details on a large map quickly. For example, in the case of the zoo map in Fig. 12, ask the students to locate some of the animals by using the silhouette symbols and the grid references. A game can be developed by devising clues such as:

> I am a bird.
> I can't fly.
> I live in cold places.
> Find me at H8.

Students can then make a set of clue cards which they exchange, working in pairs.

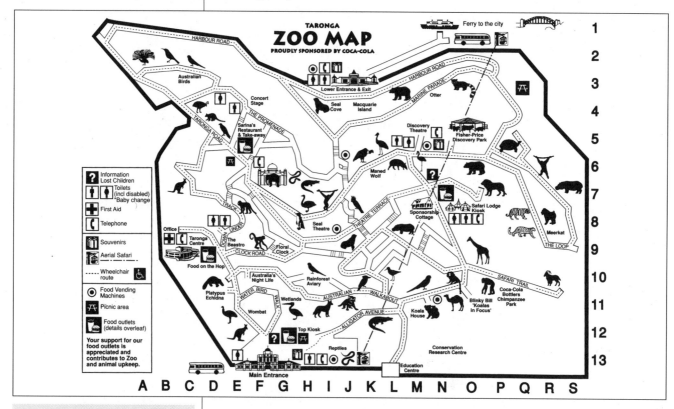

Fig. 12 ♦ Map coordinates
Ask students to find animals on the map by using the coordinates. This can be developed as a game in which pairs of students work together to locate animals by grid reference.

Most street maps are accompanied by an index which gives coordinates for each street. Give students practice at this way of accessing the map, by asking them to:

1 Look up their home street in the index and find the coordinates.
2 Use the coordinates to find their street on the map.

Maps and tables

Grids and coordinates are found in maps, graphs and tables and similar access strategies can be applied to these other forms. Coordinates were discussed in Chapter 6 "Graphs" (page 67–78) and their use in tables is discussed further in the next chapter.

Chapter 9

Tables

Although tables often have no pictorial elements, they do work as graphic texts in that the position of a word or number in a table is part of its meaning. Tables are usually made up of columns and rows, separated by rules or by white space. Each compartment inside a table is sometimes called a cell. The meaning in many tables is constructed by connecting the information in each cell with the cell's column heading and its row heading. In this respect, the way we read a table is similar to the way we read maps and graphs.

The simplest tables are *column tables*, which arrange items side by side in vertical lists. There is no significant connection between the words when they are read from left to right cross the columns (Fig. 1).

Fig. 1 ♦ A column table: "The pull of magnets" by Jaymie (grade 5)
This column table is arranged in two self-contained lists. The headings indicate that a magnet "does" or "doesn't" attract the items below.

The pull of magnets

Dose	Dosent.
Chair	table
fridge	paper
sissors	rubber
metal	pencils
Key ring	ball
paper clips	rules
taps	pencil case
car	book
stove	brick
oven	watch
bin	black board
earing	kurten.
ring	draws
tacs	bag
micawave	hair
slap band	cupet
pins	grass
neckalase	glass
heater	jumper
chain	jeans
plate	alastics
fork	cardbord
spoun	
button	
zip	

More complex are *row-and-column tables*, which arrange information in horizontal rows as well as vertical columns (Fig. 2). In this kind of table each item in the table makes a grammar-like connection between its row heading and its column heading.

Other Planets' Climates + Weather	Venus	Mars	Pluto
• Temperature	Boiling hot	Below freezing.	Below freezing.
• Wind	Gale-force winds all year	Strong winds. Seasonal dust storms.	none
• Moisture	Acid rain.	Usually none. (occasional fog.)	none
• Cloud	Dark clouds all day.	Some light clouds.	none
• Other features	Always dark. LIGHTNING. Heavy atmosphere.	Pale pink sky. Beautiful sunsets.	Starry sky all day.

Fig. 2 ♦ A row-and-column table: "Other Planets' Climate and Weather" Each item (or cell) in a row-and-column table makes a grammar-like connection between its row heading and its column heading.

Introducing tables

Interpreting tables

We can help students to interpret a table (such as "Other Planets' Climates and Weather", Fig. 2) by drawing their attention to its text elements and explaining that:

- The column headings ("Venus", "Mars" and "Pluto") give the context for each of the cells below them.
- The row headings ("Temperature", "Wind" etc.) define the theme for each cell in the row.
- We make the meaning by linking the cell's information with its row and column headings. For example, the cell "Below freezing" has the headings "Pluto" and "Temperature": we can combine these by writing, "The temperature of Pluto is below freezing".

Invite the students to interpret the table by asking questions, for example:

- You have to design a settlement on one of these planets which is self-sufficient in its energy use. Which ones are best suited to being driven by solar power or wind power?

Writing a column table

1 Jaymie's teacher provided a number of magnets and asked the students to investigate which items in the room were attracted by the magnet and which items seemed not to be affected.

2 The students were also shown examples of how a column table is arranged and were requested to arrange their findings in this form. Jaymie's table (Fig. 1, page 107) lists in two columns those items which the magnet "does" attract and those items which it "doesn't" attract. The text uses ruled lines to separate the columns and indicates which words are to be interpreted as column headings (and subheadings) by separating them from the other words with boxes. The table's main heading, "The pull of magnets", is coloured (in the original) to distinguish it from the subheadings that label the two columns.

Jaymie's text is a simple two-column table, since it does not make any significant connections between the items when they are read across the page from left to right. The text could in other words be thought of as two self-contained lists, written down side by side.

3 On completion of the table, students can exchange texts and interpret each other's results. Jaymie's text, for example, invites us to make some further connections, groupings and inferences:

- What do the items in the first column have in common that distinguishes them from those in the second column?
- What would the bin, the earring, the necklace or the plate (in the first column) be made of, to be attracted by the magnet?
- If they had been made of other materials (a cane bin, a pearl earring, a bead necklace, a china plate), would they still belong in this column?
- Can we divide the second column up into further groups (such as animal, plant or mineral)?

Writing a row-and-column table

You can introduce tables to young children by asking them to make one using real objects.

1 Ask each of the students to find an object in the room (or from home) that is "the size of your hand or smaller".

2 The students place them on the floor and discuss "which other ones belong with this one?". The items can be grouped:

- by colour and texture
- by size and shape
- by purpose (used for writing, for measuring, for cooking etc.)
- by place (found in the kitchen, in the garden etc.)
- by origin (animal, plant, mineral or plastic).

3 The students group the objects in categories. On a large sheet of paper, draw up a blank table which uses some of the categories you have discussed; these categories can be column headings or row headings.

4 Suppose you have chosen to group the items by origin. Ask the students to place the objects in their correct categories on the table. Explain that the item must belong with both its row heading and its column heading, for example, the coin is mineral/artificial, not mineral/natural. You will arrive at a classification table of real objects such as in Fig. 3A.

Figs. 3A and 3B ♦ A sorting table with real objects
You can introduce the idea of a row-and-column table to young children by setting up a sorting table, arranged in rows and columns. The students are asked to place each object where it belongs, paying attention to both the column heading and the row heading. Later, the objects can be removed from the table and their names written into the vacated spaces.

Fig. 3A ♦ Draw up a table on a large sheet of paper and add real objects to it.

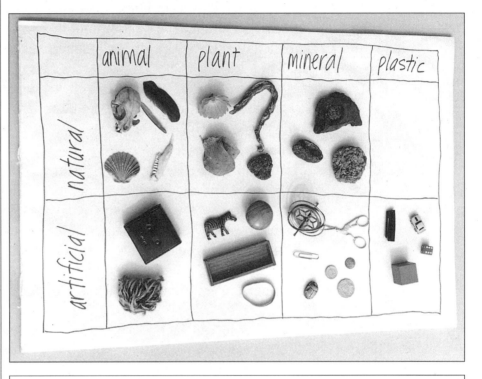

Fig. 3B ♦ As each object is removed, write its name into the table.

	animal	plant	mineral	plastic
natural	cat skull hen feather finch feather cockle shell walaby jaw	marigold flower twig jacaranda pod wood with borer holes	rock with fossil geode with crystals granite rock	
artificial	leather wallet ball of wool	wooden zebra door knob pencil box rubber band	gyroscope scissors paper clip coins clay scarab	pen cap toy car die block

5 Discuss some of the students' questions and dilemmas. For example, a living zebra is animal/natural, but a wooden carving of a zebra is plant/artificial. The shell fossil was once an animal, but has become mineralised. Discuss why there is no item in the category plastic/natural.

6 Now ask students to remove the items one by one and to write in their names as each real object is removed. The result is a table as one might find in a science book (Fig. 3B).

This activity allows students to see that a table organises information and has to be thoughtfully constructed, since the position of each object (or each name) is part of its meaning in a table.

Working with tables

"Other Planets' Climates and Weather" (Fig. 2, page 108) is a table scribed by the teacher on a large sheet of paper during a whole-class discussion, after reading a book about the planets. The information in the table was added while scanning the text for key phrases in the reference book. This is a row-and-column table, which has headings for the rows down the left hand side, as well as headings for the columns across the top. The column headings are distinguished typographically by being written in heavier (bold) type; the row headings are distinguished by being underlined and highlighted with bullets.

A table not only summarises information; it also organises it for us. This can be an advantage when we are searching for very specific information and it aids the scanning process. In order to help students see how information changes when we change its form, it is useful to ask the students to write out (as a paragraph of verbal text) some of the information from the table. The text may look something like this:

Whereas the temperature on Venus is boiling hot, it is below freezing on Mars and Pluto. Venus and Mars have strong winds as well, yet on Pluto there is no wind at all. Pluto has no rain or clouds, either; but on Mars you can get occasional fog and light clouds, while on Venus the clouds are dark all day and they produce acid rain and lightning. Mars has a pink sky, but on Pluto the stars shine all day...

Ask the students to consider what the form of the table gives us that is not in the verbal account. Most of the table's information is also in the paragraph; but the difference in form means that the way we access the information is very different. In the table it is easier to compare values for each category, to scan the text to locate the piece of data we need, to rank and organise information and to hold in mind an image of the information—that is, to remember its place in the pattern. All of these things are much harder to do when we read the paragraph which recomposes the same information in sentences. This is because the table is a more open text than the paragraph. In the table we are free to choose our own pathways through the text and to select our own priorities among the data. In this respect, the table is a more open, a more "transparent" research source than the paragraph.

Tables with figures

In the case of "The planets" (Fig. 4) the rows and columns work as they do in Fig. 2, but they include figures as well as words. While this table has spaces instead of lines to separate the rows and columns, the coordinate arrangement of the table is also similar to Fig. 2. The column headings are typographically distinguished from the data by being set in italic type; the row headings are set in bold type. The table's first-level heading "The planets" is also distinguished from all the other words in the text by its size.

Fig. 4 ♦ A table with words and figures: "The planets"
Reference books in science, history and other subjects include tables with many of the features shown here: a mixture of words and figures, a mixture of measurement units, symbols to indicate "nil" or "insignificant" and explanations of the data built into the headings.

The planets

	Average distance from Sun (million km)	*Equator diameter (km)*	*Number of moons*
Mercury	58	4 878	—
Venus	108	12 103	—
Earth	150	12 756	1
Mars	228	6 794	2
Jupiter	778	142 800	16
Saturn	1 427	120 660	23
Uranus	2 869	51 400	15
Neptune	4 497	49 400	8
Pluto	5 900	2 280	1

There is also a kind of key built into the subheadings. The words in parentheses ("million km" and "km") in the first two columns explain how to make sense of the data in those columns. We need to read the subheadings carefully, because there are three different units of measurement in these three columns.

The symbol "—" indicates zero in this table. In other tables with figures this mark may indicate "less than one" or "too small to measure" or "unknown". Also in other figure tables a final row may show totals for each column; in this table, however, to total the first and second columns would be unhelpful.

Pictorial tables

Some tables include additional visual elements which can contribute to the text's meaning. For example, the text in Fig. 5 is derived from the back of a packet of seeds. This text is a set of instructions about when and where to plant seeds and the reader therefore needs to know "where am I in the picture?" in order to follow the instructions. The instructions are therefore arranged as a table with a map built into its table structure: the map element defines the meanings of the row labels "Tropical", "Subtropical" and "Temperate". The map is a more concise way of doing this than any verbal substitute for it. Help the students to interpret a text like this by asking:

* Where are we on the map?
* Which zone do we need to read about?
* The date today is —, so is this the best time to plant? How long do we have to wait? etc.

Fig. 5 ♦ A pictorial table
These instructions, summarised from the back of a seed packet, include a map which defines the row labels in the table.

ZONES	ZONAL SOWING PERIODS	SEASON	BEST MONTHS
		Mid-Summer to early Winter	February–May
Tropical		Mid-Summer to early Winter	February–May
Subtropical		Autumn & early Spring	March April & September
Temperate			

When to sow nasturtiums

Using tables for other purposes

Tables can be used for many purposes. For example, "When to sow nasturtiums" (Fig. 5) is an instructional text. Other tables can be used to plan events (as in a train schedule). Tables can help us to organise ideas in order to make a decision. For example, as part of a technology unit on building materials, one group of students was set the task of choosing the best building material for a tree house. They were shown an example of a row-and-column table as a suitable form in which to organise the information on which they would base their decision.

The table which they produced (Fig. 6) lists the advantages and weaknesses of four kinds of materials in rows and columns, allowing the reader to compare and rank results in each category. The students selected which materials to investigate (concrete, steel, wood and cardboard: the column headings) and also chose the questions they needed to answer in order to make a decision (strong? cheap? available? etc.: the row headings).

What is the best building material for a tree house?

	concrete	steel	wood	cardboard
strong, supports weight?	✓ but very heavy	✓	✓	.
cheap and available?			✓ we have some already	✓✓
you can cut it with:	a circular saw made of carbon steel	an oxyacetylene torch	ordinary hand saw	scissors knife
easy to cut? / you join it with:	cement	welding equipment	nails, hammer, screw s/driver, drill.	✓ glue, sticky tape.
easy to join? / effect on tree	could break smaller branches.	? none	✓ nails may cause minor damage.	✓✓ no effect
effect of weather	extreme heat + cold will cause cracks.	rust (in rain)	warp planks	will rot, tear, bend, collapse.

Decision: no material is perfect, but wood is strong, available, easy to cut/join, friendly to tree + fairly resistant to rain etc.

Arranging the topics and questions in this way enabled the students to look across each row to compare the four materials' strength, cost, availability etc.; and they could look down each column to see which material "scored" best overall. Unlike a simple list or a column table, this row-and-column table organises the data, which in turn helps the students to make an informed decision.

Choosing the most useful text

When the students are preparing a report, explanation or argument, it is helpful to ask which form the information should take:

- Should we design this description as paragraphed text, as a table or in some other format?
- Can we explain this information more economically or clearly by writing it as a table?
- Can we persuade the reader to accept our argument if we list our main points as a table? etc.

It is an advantage if you have on display examples of some of these alternative texts about which the students need to make their decision. Tables can sometimes be found in big books; a form which allows all the class to view the text together. Similarly, some computer spreadsheet programs allow the user to keyboard the information as a table (or spreadsheet) and then to transform it into a graph, such as a bar, column, line or pie graph. These computer programs are usually sold as accounting or business software, rather than "educational" software; however, they do have the educational value of showing students very simply how information can be recomposed in different forms and how some of the information changes depending on the format in which it is presented. Some of these differences are:

- certain aspects of the data are more accessible in one form than in others
- the numerical values of some data may be calculated or compared more easily in one form than in another
- sometimes certain data are added or omitted, when recomposed in a different form.

Recomposing information from a table into a graph

What happens to the information in a table when we recompose it as a graph? By changing the form of the information we alter the emphasis it makes on parts of the data and the information becomes more (or less) accessible when its form is altered. More surprisingly, some of the information can actually disappear. For example, two graphs were produced using spreadsheet/graphics software, based on the information in "Number of moons" in the "The planets" table in Fig. 4, page 113. The first of these was a column graph (Fig. 7), which is ideal for conveying the relative values for each planet.

Fig. 7 ♦ A column graph based on "The planets" table

The information about moons (column 3 in Fig. 4) has been recomposed as a column graph, using ClarisWorks spreadsheet software. The graph shows relative values more clearly than the table; the table shows exact quantities more clearly than the graph.

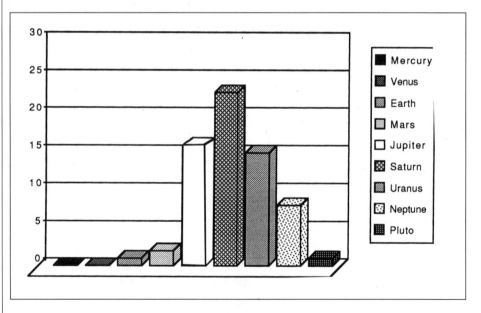

However, because the graph marks off the grid in units of five, the exact number of moons is less easy to access. On the other hand, the table exactly identifies each of these values, yet "buries" the relative differences in its column of figures. Each form, in other words, has its advantages and weaknesses; the table is more exact, while the graph communicates relative values more strongly and memorably.

The same data was also recomposed in the form of a pie graph (Fig. 8). Although this text also communicates relative differences well, the reader will not find Mercury or Venus in the graph at all, even though it is listed in the key, since pie graphs (unlike column graphs) do not record zero values. In addition, although the pie graph has shown us each planet's share of the total number of moons, it gives us no clue to the actual number of moons for each planet or the total number of moons.

Fig. 8 ♦ A pie graph based on "The planets" table
Here the same information about moons (column 3 in Fig. 4) has been recomposed as a pie graph. Some of the data in the table (for Mercury and Venus) do not appear in this graph, because pie graphs do not record zero quantities.

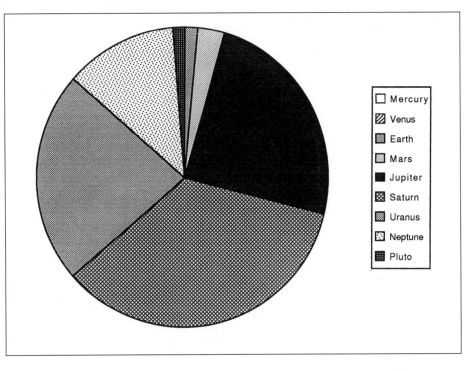

In choosing the format in which information is presented, therefore, students need to spend time discussing the relative merits of different kinds of text, the purposes of the writing exercise and the central message to be communicated. The advantage of a spreadsheet/graphic program lies in the fact that we can change the format of the information from table to graph and back again simply by "clicking OK" with a mouse and this convenience allows students to see the relative advantages or weaknesses of these different kinds of graphic text instantly and clearly.

If you wish to use spreadsheet software for this purpose, it may be worth inquiring whether some spreadsheet programs are already in use at your school in the principal's or secretary's office, for use in keeping school accounts or for scheduling. (Figs. 7 and 8 were produced using ClarisWorks software on a Macintosh computer.)

Putting it all together

In Chapters 3–9 we have looked closely at a variety of visual texts, at how they can be used and at how they work to make meaning. Yet it is not enough to employ these texts in isolation. If students are to take full advantage of these forms, it is necessary to look at diagrams, graphs, maps and tables in the wider context of how we design the page layout of an information book. Graphic design integrates verbal and visual elements on a page of an information book and makes important links between text elements (such as paragraphs, headings, captions and diagrams), both to organise the writer's information and to support the reader. This integrative aspect of information texts is the subject of the final chapter.

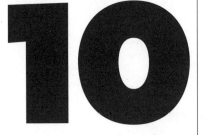

Chapter 10

Graphic design

In a publishing house the person who brings together all the elements of the book's text (the verbal or paragraphed text, the headings, the visual texts, table of contents, index etc.) is the graphic designer. Graphic design organises the information using layout and typography.

In this final chapter we look at how these elements of graphic design make an information book an integrated text. Graphic design combines visual and verbal texts and in the classroom, graphic design can be an important part of the writing process (which is also a thinking process and a visualising process).

Layout is the positioning of verbal and visual elements on the page; it includes the arrangement of paragraphs in columns, the use of headings and the positioning of visual elements next to the paragraphed text they illustrate. Layout serves to direct the reader from one part of the text to another or to provide alternative entry points (or "signposts") into the text.

Typography is the choice of type styles (such as *italic* or **bold** type) to communicate meaning, emphasis, attitude or mood. Typography helps us distinguish between main headings, subheadings and paragraphed text or between formal and informal moods in texts.

The purpose of layout and typography is to organise and to signpost information. *Signposting* combines layout and typography to direct the reader through alternative pathways in the text.

Signposts include headings, cross references, arrows, asterisks (*), leaders (..............), bullets (•) and so on. These features help the reader to locate alternative entry points and also to direct the reader to supporting information.

All of these aspects of graphic design contributes to the meaning of an information text and supports the reader in accessing the text. Knowing how to interpret these print conventions, therefore, is essential to a student's success in reading information selectively. Knowing how to employ these conventions also has a place in the writing curriculum, since the way we organise an information text is part of how we make its meaning.

For example, in "Trees' Advantages" (Fig. 1) Eugene has used some of the basic elements of layout, typography and signposting to organise his argument and to support the reader.

Fig. 1 ♦ Layout, typography and signposting: "Trees' Advantages"
Eugene (grade 3/4) has employed two levels of heading, has arranged the paragraphs in two columns and has provided alternative entry points into the text through the second-level headings.

Fig. 1 ♦ Layout, typography and signposting: "Trees' Advantages"
Eugene (grade 3/4) has employed two levels of heading, has arranged the paragraphs in two columns and has provided alternative entry points into the text through the second-level headings.

The *layout* features include:
- the arrangement of the type into two columns
- the balancing of the tree graphic as a focus for the page and as an icon-like statement of its theme.

The *typographic* features include:
- the size differentiation between the main heading ("Trees' Advantages"), the subheadings ("Leaves", "Root System" and "Futher Advantages") and the paragraphed text.

The *signposts* include:
- the subheadings, which offer alternative entry points into the paragraphed text
- the use of bullets (•) in the paragraph "Root System" to itemise a list and provide alternative entry points
- the separation by white space of the three sections of the argument to isolate the subtopics of the argument.

Layout

The layout of a published information text is not decided by chance and is not merely a matter of adding an element that is "artistic" or "decorative".

Layout has a number of functions:
- to organise information into themes or topics
- to make connections between text elements, such as between the paragraphed text and the graphics that support it
- to signal to the reader various entry points into the text.

Layout features carry out these functions by:
- arranging the paragraphed text in columns (sometimes two or three columns to the page)
- separating headings, paragraphed text, graphics etc., with boxes, rules or white space
- connecting the text elements with signposts such as arrowheads, brackets, boxes, colour, proximity etc.

Layout features include:
- rules (lines ruled or drawn across or down the page to connect or separate items)
- boxes (rectangles around a text, to highlight and separate items)
- white space (to separate items) and proximity (to link items)
- shape, position, colour and size of type and graphics (to highlight or link items)
- balancing of text elements (to give relative emphasis to parts of the text)
- aesthetic composing of visual elements (such as choice of colours, artwork style, page shape etc., to convey mood and attitude).

In the text "Growing Seeds" (Fig. 2) the student has combined a number of these layout conventions to organise the information and to support the reader. For example, the three stages of the growing process are identified as boxed graphics of equal size. These boxes separate and "fix" the stages like snapshots in a time sequence; their equal size gives the stages in the sequence equal importance. The subheadings "Dry seed", "Wet seed after 5 min." and "the next day" are distinguished from the caption text by their position inside the boxes and each subheading is separated from the graphic inside its box by a rule.

Fig. 2 ♦ Layout features: "Growing Seeds"
The student (grade 5) has used layout features such as boxes, rules and white space to organise the information and to support the reader.

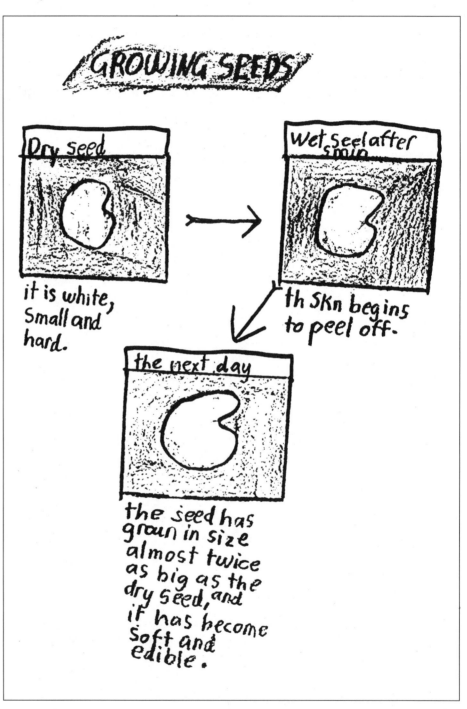

The captions (such as "it is white, small and hard") are identified as different from the headings because they fall outside of and below each box. Each caption is linked to its box by proximity (closeness) and each caption floats together with its boxed graphic as an island of text separated by white space from the other two graphics-with-captions. Although they are separated in this way, the three graphics are joined by arrows, which help both to integrate the text and to indicate the direction in which we should read it.

These layout features are supported by the text's typography: for example, the caption type is aligned "flush left" (the words are lined up on the left side only) connecting it with the left edge of the box to which it belongs. The main heading "Growing Seeds" is identified by being written in the largest type and is the only type (in the original) on a coloured background. Typography and layout are usually linked in this way to organise meanings in graphic texts.

Text positioning

The positioning of the words in a text includes paragraphing, indenting, alignment and so on. Text positioning supports both the writer and the reader by:

- helping the writer to organise the information
- assisting or directing the reader to sort through the information.

Paragraphing

Students are traditionally instructed to indent paragraphs; that is to "start a new paragraph by leaving a space". This is also a widely used convention in published books. However, books generally do not indent the first paragraph that follows a heading (that is, the paragraph that starts a new chapter or a new section of a chapter).

Indented quotations

Students are also often told that all direct quotations are to be enclosed in quotation marks (" "). However, in most printed books direct quotations that are more than two or three lines long are presented as indented blocks of type:

> Students are also usually told that all direct quotations are to be enclosed in quotation marks (" "). However, in most printed books direct quotations that are more than two or three lines long are presented as indented blocks of type.

Sometimes, though not always, these lines are set in a smaller typeface, as shown in the above example.

Typography

Typography (the choice of type styles) contributes to the meaning and organisation of a text by:

- ranking the importance of topics and subtopics of information
- providing alternative entry points into the text
- signposting alternative pathways through the text
- directing the reader to additional, supporting information
- conveying emphasis, attitude (to the subject or to the reader) and mood.

Type can come in many different styles, called typefaces and fonts.

Typefaces

A text can be typeset in different typefaces such as:

Times	a "serious" typeface used in newspapers and books
Tekton	a "freehand" typeface used in advertising
Helvetica compressed	a typeface used for packaging.

Typefaces like Times are often used for extended passages of paragraphed text (such as reference works, newspaper articles, encyclopaedias), whereas typefaces like Tekton and Helvetica are usually reserved for shorter texts (such as advertising, magazine headings, brochure texts, display posters etc.). The choice of typeface can also convey mood, attitude and emphasis. Formal typefaces are sometimes used to attribute importance to its subject and sometimes to seek a respectful attitude in the reader. Informal typefaces, on the other hand, often suggest a more relaxed and equal relationship between writer and reader.

Typography can also convey the writer's attitude to the subject. For example, the title page of a book on toxic waste (Fig. 3A) conveys through the choice of type design not only the subject's possible texture, but also its menace; and the important place of nuclear waste within the larger theme of toxic waste is conveyed in superimposing a radiation symbol over one of the letters. The effect

Figs. 3A and 3B ♦ Using typography

Fig. 3A ♦ Creating mood and attitude with typography
For his title page of a book about toxic waste Hugo (grade 6) has used typography to convey his attitude to the subject and to emphasise the importance of nuclear waste within the broader topic of toxic waste.

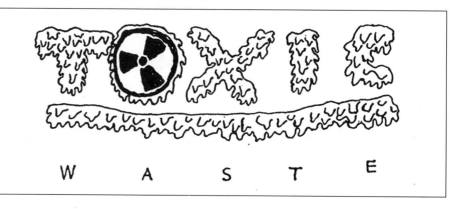

is that even before we start reading we are prepared for the writer's attitude to his theme and the attitude he seeks to establish in the reader.

Students who use word processors in the classroom have access to a range of typefaces which they can use in their writing. Other students can hand-letter the typefaces they want, using books, newspapers and other printed material as references.

Fonts

Most typefaces have at least three fonts:

roman	which is the standard style for most texts
italic	which is used for highlighting key words or the names of books or some scientific terms
bold	which is a heavier, blacker style often used for main headings, strong emphasis or warnings etc.

These fonts are found in most information texts such as reference books and they can be used by students who have access to word processing software. In students' handwritten texts:

italic	can be represented by <u>underlining</u>.
bold	can be represented by outlining.

Students can use these underline and outline conventions to indicate headings and emphasised words, while the use of a thick marker pen for headings is a common handwritten form of bold type (Fig. 3B).

Working with layout and typography

We see a number of the features of both typography and layout used together in the text "CROSS SECTIONS" (Fig. 4) by a group of grade 5/6 students.

Fig. 4 ♦ Layout and typography: "Cross Sections"
A group of grade 5/6 students produced this text which shows three levels of headings and a variety of typographic and layout elements.

The main heading (or first-level heading) "CROSS SECTIONS" has been given prominence typographically as it is the only heading that has been written with a thick marker pen in bold capitals. The layout of the text has also contributed to this prominence, since the heading is positioned so as to refer to both of the boxed graphics "KIWI fruit" and "SNOW PEAs in Pod" and has a bracketing effect subordinating the two boxed graphics to the heading.

The second-level headings "KIWI fruit" and "SNOW PEAs in Pod" are written using outlining (in a finer pen) and shading and their reference is limited to the box in which they appear.

There is also a third-level heading in each box, namely the word "Legend", which applies only to the small boxes and labels below it. The labels for each box of the legend are subordinated in size to the heading "Legend". First, second and third level headings are clearly ranked by size and this supports the reader in interpreting the nested structure of the text; that is, the legend's information falls within the graphic "KIWI fruit" which in turn falls within the theme "CROSS SECTIONS".

The two graphic texts, "KIWI fruit" and "SNOW PEAs in Pod", are at the same time joined and separated by boxes of heavy rules, indicating that these are two examples of the theme "CROSS SECTIONS". The students have been careful to use the same conventions to organise the information within each of the two boxes: for example, the two subheadings, "KIWI fruit" and "SNOW PEAs in Pod", are in the same shaded outline style and the two legends are organised with the same type size and layout. This helps the reader who, having decoded the principles of the text in the "KIWI fruit" box, can more rapidly process the information in the "SNOW PEAs in Pod" box.

Signposts

Signposts are typographic or layout features that indicate:
- an entry point into the text
- a pathway through the text.

Since the reader is not always obliged to begin information texts at the beginning, signposts (such as headings, numbers or arrows) help readers to find their way around the text. Signposts are most often used when the reader is "scanning" the text for very specific information, typically when researching a topic using an encyclopaedia or reference book.

Some common signposts include:

- **Headings and subheadings**
  These label the theme of the paragraphs which follow and in doing so offer the reader a point of entry into the stream of the writer's thinking.

- **Bullets** — a bullet has been typeset at the beginning of this line. Bullets are used to highlight each new entry point in a list of information. Using bullets helps the reader to review a list and to choose which items to read and which to pass over. Bullets are always lined up vertically down the left side of the information, as on page 128, and each bullet indicates a new entry point. Bullets are also useful when making research notes.

- **Arrows (→) and arrowheads (➤)**
  These can link items in a visual text, they can show directionality (the writer's preferred sequence of items), they can link a label to its part in a diagram or they can show entry points into the information.

- **Boxes, rules, borders and loops**
  These group items thematically and separate them from other pieces of information on the page.

- **Leaders**
  These are a row of dots (............) which are used, for example, in a table of contents, to help the eye link up chapter names with pages numbers:

  Chapter One 9
  Chapter Two 16

  Leaders direct the reader to make connections between elements in each line of text, just as arrows make connections in diagrams.

- **Asterisks (*)**
  These make connections between a part of the paragraphed text and the footnote which belongs with that part of the text. They are used to give the source of the information or to explain (as it were in a long "aside" or parenthesis) some subsidiary or supporting fact which otherwise would hold up the flow of the main text. The footnote* to which the asterisk belongs is usually placed at the foot of the same page and is sometimes separated from the paragraphed text by a rule or a space.

  ---
  * A footnote is usually typeset in a smaller typeface.

- **Footnote numbers**
  Where more than one footnote is required, the asterisk is replaced with a number, written above the line[1]. The numbered footnote can be placed either at the foot of the page or at the end of the chapter.

  ---
  [1] A footnote is usually typeset in a smaller typeface.

- **Indicators**
  These are words or symbols used in captions to link the caption to its graphic. The link can be expressed as "left", "right", "above", "top left", "below" etc. or by arrowheads (➤) and point towards the graphic to which the caption refers.

- **Cross references**
  These are instructions to the reader (usually embedded in the paragraphed text, in parentheses), which refer us to other parts

of the text which are relevant to the subject being discussed. They can begin with an instruction (see page xx) or they can simply refer to the item to be looked up (Fig. 99).

- **Defined terms**
  In some information texts a key word or phrase is highlighted in *italic* or **bold** type on the first occasion the term is used (or the occasion on which the term is defined). The defined term works as a signpost for the reader who has just turned to this page (often after consulting the index) and allows the reader to enter the stream of the writer's text at the point where this term is formally introduced.

- **Page numbers**
  These are the link between the information on any page and references to it in the table of contents, the index or a glossary etc. In order to locate page numbers quickly, they are usually placed at the top or bottom of the page, clear of the paragraphed text and set in a smaller type size. Numbers on the left pages are usually even and numbers on the right pages are usually odd. The page numbers in the index can be typeset in roman, italic or bold fonts and each font is assigned a specific meaning, as in:

  stegosaurs, 5, 11, 16–24, 17, 20–21, 39

  — The roman page numbers (5, 11, 39) usually indicate minor entries in the paragraphed text.
  — The **bold** page numbers (**16–24**) usually indicate a main entry (the longest entry or the entry in which the defined term "stegosaurs" is likely to be explained).
  — The *italic* page numbers (*17, 20–21*) sometimes indicate a graphic text (illustration, diagram, map or graph).

- **Number labels**
  These are simply the labels for a sequence of items in a text which need to be read in a certain order to make sense. Number labels can be used with any kind of text: individual words in a list, whole paragraphs, photographs, captioned graphics etc.

In Fig. 5 ("How to make a Jack in the box") Belinda (grade 5) has employed some of these signposts to organise her material and to support the reader in following the instructions. For example, she has boxed each step in the process as a separate event and has used number labels to identify each step. This design element helps the writer to organise the sequencing of the information; it also supports the reader who is following the steps in order to make the

Jack in the box, since the reader needs frequently to disengage from the text (in order to make the toy Jack in the box) and to return to the instructions at the next entry point.

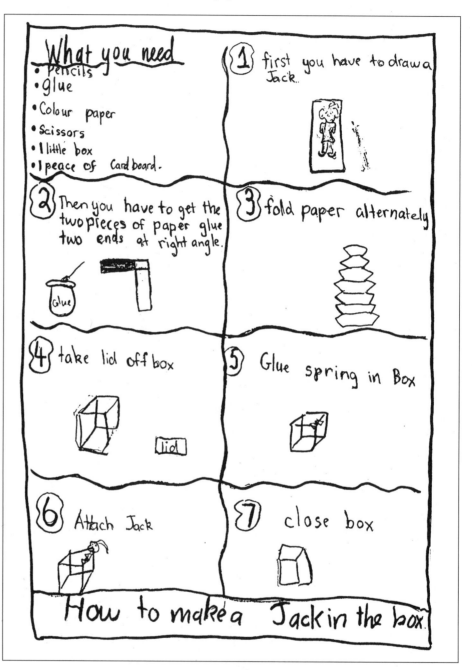

The heading ("How to make ..."), the subheading ("What you need") and the number labels (1–7) are distinguished from the instructional captions by being written in bold print (with a thicker pen), which helps the reader to find the next step easily when re-engaging with the text. Belinda has also organised the names of the materials to be used (inside the box headed "What you need") as a list of items highlighted with bullets, which assist both writer and reader to count off and check the actual materials against the list.

Graphic design in the classroom

One chapter from Hugo's book on toxic waste is reproduced in Fig. 6. This text was drafted and revised once with pen and paper, then keyboarded on a computer using a page layout program.

The typographic features here include:

- the use of a poster-style typeface, which conveys the sense of urgency already established in the book's title (Fig. 3A, page 124)
- the subheadings, "D.D.T. in the environment" and "Resistance to D.D.T." are set inside black boxes, again suggesting newspaper-style urgency
- The defined term "carcinogen" is highlighted by being typeset in italics, so that this word is easier to find if we have arrived at this page after looking up "carcinogen" in the index.

Layout features are also important in Hugo's text:

- the paragraphs are arranged in columns, newspaper-style
- the caption, "If the hawk ate the snakes ..." explains the process in the flow diagram at the foot of the page
- the diagram supports the information under the subheading "Resistance to D.D.T."

Pesticides and herbicides

Pesticides are toxic insect killers and herbicides are toxic weed killers. An example of pesticides is D.D.T.

D.D.T. in the environment

D.D.T. kills insects on crops. It was banned in the U.S.A., West Germany, France and most other industrial countries after research proved it was a *carcinogen* (cancer-causing substance). This wasn't the end of D.D.T. for birds were still found to have high levels of D.D.T. in their bodies.

D.D.T. is still being manufactured and sent to the developing countries (Third World) to use on cash crops.

Resistance to D.D.T.

Another problem with D.D.T. is that insects are building up a resistance to it which means more and more D.D.T. needs to be used. As this pesticide moves through the food chain *(see diagram below)* it becomes more concentrated. As a result one future problem is that we won't be able to eat anything that has had D.D.T. sprayed on it without getting very sick.

What can we do?

The only solutions are:
- Boycott any companies that produce D.D.T. or any other pesticide or herbicide.
- Use organic farming.

Below: D.D.T. in the food chain
If the hawk ate the snakes it would be more sick than if it ate the mouse because of the pesticide build-up in the food chain.

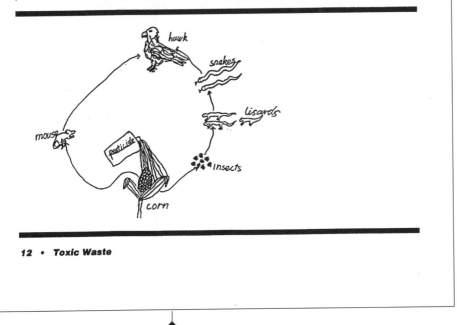

- the conclusion ("What can we do?") is given prominence by being placed inside a box with extra white space and typeset in a different typeface.

This example benefits from having been keyboarded on a computer and printed out on a laser printer. With the increasing use of desktop publishing in classrooms, students have the opportunity to experiment with the subtle messages that can be conveyed through the selection of these programs' design features. Programs which enable your students to do this range from inexpensive word processing applications such as Microsoft Word and ClarisWorks through to more costly programs such as PageMaker and QuarkXPress. However, students without access to desktop publishing can still use the principles of graphic design in handwritten texts, such as in the same student's "Science Experiment" (Fig. 7). This integrated text employs many graphic design features, including two levels of headings, boxes, rules, a picture glossary which also works as a flow diagram, labels and arrows, alignment of the text into lists and the separation of key elements using white space.

Fig. 7 ♦ "Science Experiment"
Hugo (grade 5) has used handwritten typographic elements to organise the data in his list of materials and in the instructions which follow.

SCIENCE EXPERIMENT

Hugo

A Aim: the aim of the experiment was to show which materials conduct electricity.

B Equipment: 5 alligator clips
1 light globe with wires attached
1 battery holder with wires attached
1 battery
1 piece of wire

C Materials to test: 1 two cent coin
1 twenty cent coin
1 one dollar coin
1 piece of plastic
1 piece of card board
1 piece of wood
1 piece of graphite
1 piece of glass

D Procedure: 1. Take one of the above materials
2. Put one alligator clip on each end of the material.
3. Make sure the alligator clips are not touching each other.
4. If the light globe lights up then the material conducts electricity.
5. If the light globe does not light up then the material does not conduct electricity

E Conclusion: The light globe lit up when the two cent coin, 1 twenty cent coin, 1 one dollar coin and the piece of graphite were tested. This proves that those materials conduct electricity.
The light globe did not light up when the pieces of plastic, card board, wood and glass were tested. This proves that those material do not conduct electricity.

←LIGHT GLOBE

ALLIGATOR CLIPS

GRAPHITE

- BATTERY +

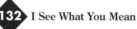

In a grade 4 classroom three students worked together to produce the text in Fig. 8. Their task was to invent a reptile which could survive in the wild, explaining their invented animal as a scientist would, using appropriate text conventions. The students modelled their text on a field guide format. The graphic design features they have employed include:

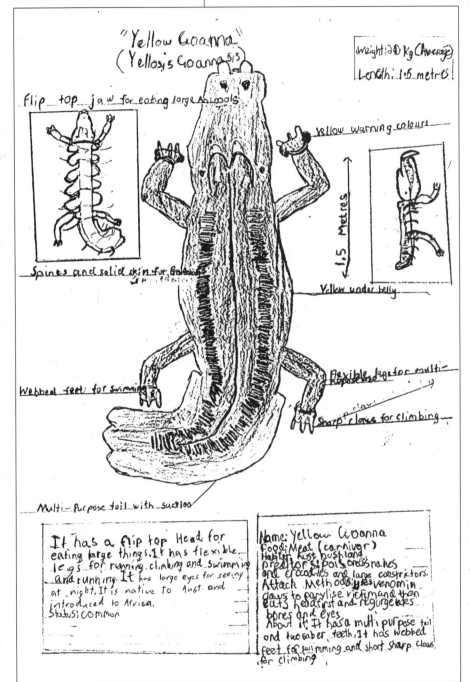

- a main heading ("Yellow Goanna") which unites all the text elements below it
- a simple diagram, which locates the animal's attributes using labels and arrows
- a boxed cutaway diagram (at left) to show the lizard's skeleton
- a boxed scale diagram (at right) showing the skeleton from a side view
- a caption (top right) indicating the animal's length and weight
- paragraphed text arranged in two columns comprising:
  — an explanation of how the lizard's attributes help it to survive (left column)
  — a list of key facts such as food, habitat, predators etc.

Graphic design and integrated texts

A graphic designer's job is to make an integrated text from the author's verbal text and the illustrator's graphics (maps, diagrams etc.). In a publishing house these separate elements are usually presented to the designer with a minimum of advice as to how they are to be combined on the page. The writer's text may make cross references to the illustrations, which are numbered to match these cross references. But the choice of sizing and positioning these elements on each page is the designer's task. The designer is also expected to make decisions about the presentation of other elements as well, including the design of:

- front and back covers
- title page
- table of contents
- index
- glossary.

All of these design tasks can be usefully demonstrated and practised in the classroom. Students need both experience and explicit instruction in how we use each of these text elements differently. For example, we read an index differently from a table of contents.

Front cover

The cover's title and graphics are scanned for orientating us in the theme of the book and for establishing expectations about its suitability for our own purposes as readers. This is the first step in a series of highly selective reading processes we use when working with information texts.

Back cover

If the back cover provides a blurb (the publisher's summary of the theme, often written by the editor), we can use this text to orientate ourselves in the book's content and to assess the extent of its scope. At this point we may decide to continue with this book or to put it aside, if it does not suit our purpose.

Title page

Usually the title page adds very little (apart from the publisher's name) to what we have already gained from the covers. Some title pages add a new graphic element which extends our expectations of the book.

Table of contents

This page lists all the chapter headings in the order in which they appear in the book, but they usually omit subheadings. The table of contents can be used to sample the book's main themes and to orientate the reader in the way the information in the book has been organised. If the theme we are looking for is a chapter heading, we can use the table of contents (which lists the first page of each chapter) to turn to the section we want.

Index

On the other hand, indexes include references to many minor details in the text, not just the major themes. The topics are arranged in alphabetical order. Like other alphabetical lists (such as a gazetteer, dictionary or phone book) we rarely if ever read the whole of an index, as we might do a table of contents. Instead, we pick out one or two lines, note the page number and access the text on those pages.

Glossary

We use a glossary while we are in the midst of reading a paragraph elsewhere in the book. Our reading pattern for glossaries is therefore different from reading either an index or a table of contents. When we encounter an unfamiliar term, we disengage from the text (while still "keeping our place") and access the glossary for this term by locating it alphabetically. We read only the paragraph in the glossary that is signposted by this term and often need to reread both the glossary entry and the paragraph before we can make full sense of the term in the paragraphed text. Finally we close the glossary and re-engage with the text where we kept our place.

Reading the design in published texts

Before students attempt their own writing, illustrating and designing of an integrated text, allow them the opportunity to look closely at some published examples. Suitable books are likely to be in your classroom already, perhaps in the form of a permanent collection of information books, books borrowed from the library or information "big books".

Examples in big books:
The Book of Animal Records
    contents page, p. 2
    introduction, p. 3
    headings, paragraphed text in 2 columns, diagrams, pp. 4–13
    glossary and abbreviations list, p. 16
    index, p. 17
Small Worlds or *The Gas Giants*
    contents page, p. 2
    introduction, p. 3
    headings and subheadings, captions, diagrams, paragraphs, pp. 4–16
    glossary and index, p. 17
Earth in Danger
    contents page, p. 2
    introduction, p. 3
    headings, paragraphed text, captions and diagrams, pp. 4–16
    bibliography and index, p. 17
    glossary, p. 18

Discuss how design problems have been handled by professional designers. This can be done as a whole-class activity led by the teacher using a big book or the students can work in small groups, using criteria such as:

- Can I find what I want to know easily and quickly?
- Does the layout help me to read it?
- Do the headings stand out, so that I know where to look for information?

Fig. 9 ♦ Graphic design in published books
In this double-page spread from Michael Benton's *The Story of Life on Earth*, a professional graphic designer has organised the paragraphed text (the main body of the verbal text) and visual texts on the page into an integrated text.

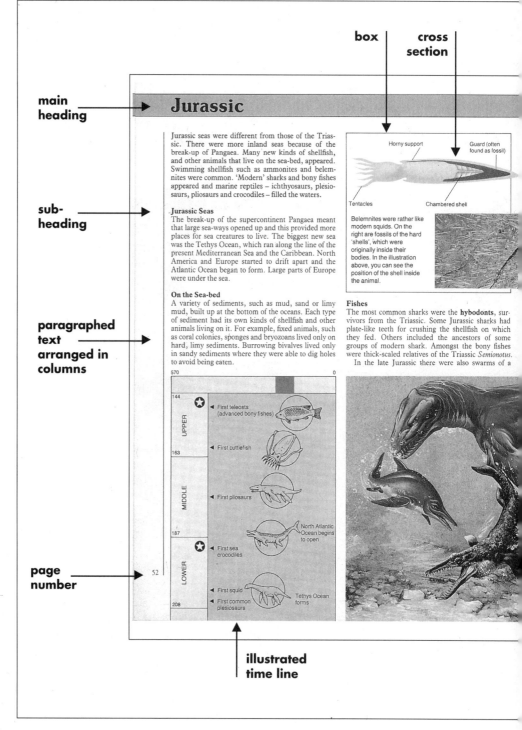

box

cross section

main heading

Jurassic

Jurassic seas were different from those of the Triassic. There were more inland seas because of the break-up of Pangaea. Many new kinds of shellfish, and other animals that live on the sea-bed, appeared. Swimming shellfish such as ammonites and belemnites were common. 'Modern' sharks and bony fishes appeared and marine reptiles – ichthyosaurs, plesiosaurs, pliosaurs and crocodiles – filled the waters.

sub-heading

Jurassic Seas
The break-up of the supercontinent Pangaea meant that large sea-ways opened up and this provided more places for sea creatures to live. The biggest new sea was the Tethys Ocean, which ran along the line of the present Mediterranean Sea and the Caribbean. North America and Europe started to drift apart and the Atlantic Ocean began to form. Large parts of Europe were under the sea.

On the Sea-bed
A variety of sediments, such as mud, sand or limy mud, built up at the bottom of the oceans. Each type of sediment had its own kinds of shellfish and other animals living on it. For example, fixed animals, such as coral colonies, sponges and bryozoans lived only on hard, limy sediments. Burrowing bivalves lived only in sandy sediments where they were able to dig holes to avoid being eaten.

paragraphed text arranged in columns

Horny support

Guard (often found as fossil)

Tentacles

Chambered shell

Belemnites were rather like modern squids. On the right are fossils of the hard 'shells', which were originally inside their bodies. In the illustration above, you can see the position of the shell inside the animal.

Fishes
The most common sharks were the **hybodonts**, survivors from the Triassic. Some Jurassic sharks had plate-like teeth for crushing the shellfish on which they fed. Others included the ancestors of some groups of modern shark. Amongst the bony fishes were thick-scaled relatives of the Triassic *Semionotus*. In the late Jurassic there were also swarms of a

570

0

144

UPPER

◄ First teleosts (advanced bony fishes)

◄ First cuttlefish

163

MIDDLE

◄ First pliosaurs

187

North Atlantic Ocean begins to open

◄ First sea crocodiles

page number

52

LOWER

◄ First squid

◄ First common plesiosaurs

Tethys Ocean forms

208

illustrated time line

- Do the graphics add information or are they just decorative, empty or repetitious?
- Do the captions add to the paragraphed text or just repeat it?
- Can I locate key words and images easily?
- Can I find my way around the page or is it cluttered, crammed or confusing?
- How does the design help me to find the information I need?
- How would I have done it better?

For example, Fig. 9 reproduces two pages from a book for young readers about prehistoric life. In this double-page spread a professional graphic designer has arranged the paragraphed text and the visual texts using these design features:

- a main heading ("Jurassic ... 208–144 million years ago") which unites all the text elements under it
- subheadings ("Jurassic Seas" etc.) each of which signposts the theme of the paragraphs that follow it
- paragraphs arranged in columns
- defined terms (such as "pliosaurs") highlighted in bold type
- a box which links the cross section with its explanatory caption (Belemnites were rather like modern squids ...")
- a numbered key (1–9 at lower right) which identifies the names of the animals in the drawing by referring to their outlines in the picture glossary.

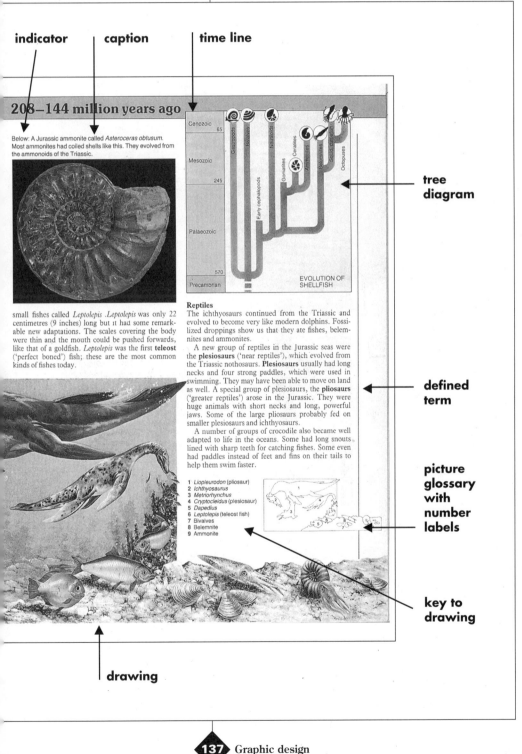

indicator   caption   time line

208–144 million years ago

Below: A Jurassic ammonite called *Asteroceras obtusum*. Most ammonites had coiled shells like this. They evolved from the ammonoids of the Triassic.

EVOLUTION OF SHELLFISH

tree diagram

small fishes called *Leptolepis* .*Leptolepis* was only 22 centimetres (9 inches) long but it had some remarkable new adaptations. The scales covering the body were thin and the mouth could be pushed forwards, like that of a goldfish. *Leptolepis* was the first **teleost** ('perfect boned') fish; these are the most common kinds of fishes today.

Reptiles
The ichthyosaurs continued from the Triassic and evolved to become very like modern dolphins. Fossilized droppings show us that they ate fishes, belemnites and ammonites.

A new group of reptiles in the Jurassic seas were the **plesiosaurs** ('near reptiles'), which evolved from the Triassic nothosaurs. **Plesiosaurs** usually had long necks and four strong paddles, which were used in swimming. They may have been able to move on land as well. A special group of plesiosaurs, the **pliosaurs** ('greater reptiles') arose in the Jurassic. They were huge animals with short necks and long, powerful jaws. Some of the large pliosaurs probably fed on smaller plesiosaurs and ichthyosaurs.

A number of groups of crocodile also became well adapted to life in the oceans. Some had long snouts lined with sharp teeth for catching fishes. Some even had paddles instead of feet and fins on their tails to help them swim faster.

defined term

1 *Liopleurodon* (pliosaur)
2 *Ichthyosaurus*
3 *Metriorhynchus*
4 *Cryptocleidus* (plesiosaur)
5 *Dapedius*
6 *Leptolepis* (teleost fish)
7 Bivalves
8 Belemnite
9 Ammonite

picture glossary with number labels

key to drawing

drawing

Graphic design serves the purpose of integrating the text; that is, making connections between the words, the diagrams, the headings and the other small details such as cross references, footnotes and page numbers. Some of the more important connections that are typically found in the page design of an illustrated information book are shown in Fig. 10.

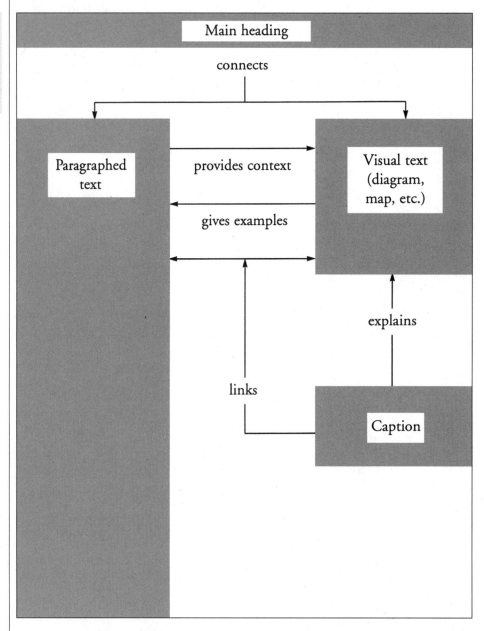

Graphic design: a suggested teaching strategy

1 Show the students examples of integrated texts, by bringing illustrated reference books into the classroom.

2 Use an information "big book" to show some of the key features of an integrated text, such as table of contents, glossary, index, headings, graphics, captions etc.

3 Point out these features in a meaningful context, for example to answer the students' own questions. Before opening the book, act as scribe for the students to make a table on a large sheet of paper under headings such as:

Topic:		
We know	We're not sure about	We need to know

Scan the text for answers to the students' questions, using the index, page numbers, headings, graphics and paragraphed text. Point out these features only in the context of helping the students answer their questions.

4 Ask the students to write "another page to go in the book", or:

5 Ask the students to work in groups to write their own book. Each group of students works on one or two pages of the book. The book must be on a topic of their own choice. Share out the tasks, such as:

Group 1 — title page, table of contents
Group 2 — introduction
Group 3 — chapter 1 / topic one
Group 4 — chapter 2 / topic two
... etc. ...
Group 9 — glossary, abbreviations
Group 10 — index

6 The theme of the book should be decided by the whole class. During discussion, the students brainstorm themes and issues to be covered, make notes of this discussion and decide on the best sequence in which to arrange the topics. Assign themes to each group.

7 Sources: the students can conduct their research using:
- other books
- photographs
- interviews
- data banks
- letters to other information sources
- their own prior knowledge, pooled in each group.

Some topics to start with
Younger children (years K–2)
Younger children can successfully research a topic such as:
- our pets
- thirty years ago
- places we have visited,

using only the group's prior knowledge or a visitor to the classroom and a tape recorder or postcards and colour photographs as resources. This limits the amount of words-only reading that they will need to do, while still developing reference and research skills such as attention to detail, checking hypotheses against sources, selective reading (of pictures), comparing alternate sources of information etc.

Topics for younger children might, for example, include:

- *Pet care and record book* — each group researches their own pets under headings such as size, feeding, care, protection, enclosure, exercise needs etc. Records can include the smallest, largest, smartest, longest living, hungriest, fastest running or the most unusual pet owned by Grade 1 etc. Each page can be illustrated with drawings or photographs, scale diagrams, picture glossaries and time lines.

- *Thirty years ago* — invite an adult to talk to the students about their childhood "thirty years ago" and tape record the visit; or encourage the students to tape record an interview with a parent or relative. Prepare a list of questions beforehand. Replay the interview tape in class. Act as scribe for the students by making notes on a flip chart, organising the information under headings. Each group of students works on a separate topic and collects or draws visual texts such as photographs, diagrams, time lines and maps.

- *A geography of "places we have visited"* — can be produced by interviewing one another in the group and can be illustrated with maps, drawings, postcards and time lines.

Older students (years 3–8)

These students can use a wider range of reference materials: books, magazines, newspapers, information gained by writing letters to a museum, the zoo or a local business etc.

Topics for older students might include:

- *Our town: a visitor's guide* — the students need to consider what a person needs to know on a first visit to their suburb or town. Topics could include: accommodation, local transport, restaurants, movies, shopping, recreation etc. They also need to consider the best design for each topic: an alphabetical list might suit some topics (such as emergency phone numbers), whereas a table might be better for others (such as a bus timetable). Several topics would need to be accompanied by a map. Photographs of local landmarks could be collected in the form of postcards or the students could photograph or draw them. Students will need to collect travel brochures both for information and as examples of graphic design.

- *Mars cities* — the students design a number of life-supporting cities for Mars (or another planet of the students' choice), based on information about the planet which they can research in reference books. The cities would have to meet our needs for temperature control, air, water, aesthetic and emotional needs, travel, environmental protection, sport and recreation, scientific observations etc. The text could include maps, photographs, drawings, captions, diagrams, cross sections, cutaways, tables and block diagrams.

- *Dinosaurs: an owner's guide* — the students design and write a practical guide on how to care for a pet dinosaur. The information in the book must be as close as possible to the facts as we know them; where information seems unavailable, the hypotheses need to be plausible. The students choose a dinosaur and research it under subheadings such as feeding, grooming, shelter and protection from predators, exercise, preferred habitat, life expectancy etc. Graphics might include picture glossaries, scale diagrams (showing size or mass), life cycle diagrams, tables (of feeding times and pet care), maps (of habitats) etc.

- *"The Ancient Times"* — the students write and design a newspaper dated two or three thousand years ago and set in Rome or Egypt, including news, classified advertising, weather reports, sports page, theatre and music reviews, letters to the editor etc. Graphics could include drawings (news "photographs"), weather maps, display advertising, political cartoons etc.

Keep it simple

When introducing graphic design activities, keep the tasks simple, for example:

- start with simple and short tasks (one topic, one page, one session)
- allow students to specialise on aspects of the text they are best at (some may be better at illustration, research, writing, editing or design etc.)
- allow students to become familiar with small tasks (a map or a cross section) before attempting larger ones
- the purpose of this activity is to make meaning and to investigate a topic; it is *not* busy work in "learning graphic design".

To provide a variety of experiences, it is also suggested that:

- the tasks of researcher, author, editor, illustrator and designer could be rotated (each student attempts a different role on a different day)
- students can work in pairs (as joint researchers or joint authors etc.) to share the load and support each other
- the task should always be concluded within a day or two, even if some elements are not completed

- the themes and topics should be of the students' own choosing and should be of genuine interest to them.

Some students can work more successfully alone. While this strategy allows for both individual work and group collaboration, some individuals on some occasions prefer to take responsibility for all the elements in their text, as researcher, author, illustrator, editor and designer.

Teaching practices: graphic design

- Identify different graphic designs in reference books and ask students whether the page layout and typography help us to interpret the texts more fully, rapidly and appropriately.
- Encourage students to recognise and make use of signposts that assist us in finding and accessing information.
- Show students how indexes and tables of contents help them to use their reference skills such as scanning a text for information.
- Vary and extend the forms in which students can make notes when scanning and collecting information (by using, for example, tables and graphs in addition to simple lists).
- Allow students to design their texts, not simply to write them.
- Encourage students to sort and organise their ideas (using layout elements such as boxes, arrows and headings) when writing information texts.
- Ask students, "Will the meaning be clearer if we express it as a diagram (map, table etc.) instead of as a paragraphed text?".
- Help students to assess the design of the texts they read. Is it designed for clarity, economy, impact? Is the design helpful? Is it persuasive?
- Demonstrate (using an information big book) how signposting helps us to select and focus on the specific information that we need in order to complete a research task.

Bibliography

Big Books

Bolton, F. and E. Cullen. 1996. *Animal Shelters*. Greenvale, NY: Mondo.

Brian, J. 1991. *Amazing Landforms*. Adelaide, Australia: Era Publications.

————. 1991. *Natural Disasters*. Adelaide, Australia: Era Publications.

Churchett, G. 1992. *Rainforests of Australia*. Melbourne, Australia: Rigby Heinemann.

Croser, J. 1989. *Keeping Silkworms*. Adelaide, Australia: Era Publications.

Drew, D. 1987. *The Book of Animal Records*. Crystal Lake, IL: Rigby.

————. 1987. *Caterpillar Diary*. Crystal Lake, IL: Rigby.

————. 1987. *The Life of the Butterfly*. Crystal Lake, IL: Rigby.

————. 1987. *Tadpole Diary*. Crystal Lake, IL: Rigby.

————. 1988. *Hidden Animals*. Crystal Lake, IL: Rigby.

————. 1988. *Millions of Years Ago*. Crystal Lake, IL: Rigby.

————. 1988. *Somewhere in the Universe*. Crystal Lake, IL: Rigby.

————. 1988. *What Did You Eat Today?* Crystal Lake, IL: Rigby.

————. 1989. *Body Maps*. Crystal Lake, IL: Rigby.

————. 1989. *The Gas Giants*. Crystal Lake, IL: Rigby.

————. 1989. *Small Worlds*. Crystal Lake, IL: Rigby.

————. 1990. *Animal Acrobats*. Crystal Lake, IL: Rigby.

————. 1990. *Earth in Danger*. Crystal Lake, IL: Rigby.

————. 1992. *Alone in the Desert*. Crystal Lake, IL: Rigby.

————. 1992. *The Cat on the Chimney*. Crystal Lake, IL: Rigby.

————. 1992. *What Should I Use?* Crystal Lake, IL: Rigby.

————. 1993. *Misbuildings*. Crystal Lake, IL: Rigby.

————. 1993. *Toy Designer*. Crystal Lake, IL: Rigby.

Green, R. 1996. *Caterpillars*. Greenvale, NY: Mondo.

Howes, J. 1987. *Five Trees*. Melbourne, Australia: Macmillan.

Jacaranda Atlas Programme. 1983. *Moving into Maps*. Jacaranda, Australia: Jacaranda Wiley.

Kelly, A. 1992. *Looking at Maps*. Crystal Lake, IL: Rigby.

Ollier, C. 1993. *Australia: An Ancient Land*. Gosford, Australia: Scholastic Australia.

Tyler, M. 1992. *Earthworms*. Gosford, Australia: Scholastic Australia.

CD-ROM

Dorling Kindersley. 1994. *Stephen Biesty's Incredible Cross Sections: Stowaway!* PC or Macintosh. Boston: distributed by Houghton Mifflin.

Dorling Kindersley. 1994. *The Ultimate Human Body*. PC or Macintosh. Boston: distributed by Houghton Mifflin.

Index